Geri-Active

by Steve Carrier
Copyright 2022, all rights reserved
stevecarrier02@gmail.com

No part of this book may be reproduced, stored in a retrieval system or transmitted by any means without written permission of the author

Acknowledgments

Thank you, Marc, for encouragement, and Darryl for caring about spelling and punctuation and Joe for being the youngest old guy I know and Doug who gave me good stuff. Finally, thanks Val. Always, Val.

Cover photo:

Photo is by granddaughter Jacey. Playing first base is grandson Hunter. Pitching is grandson-in-law Austin. Umpiring is son Jeff and taking a dangerous lead off first base is – me and my mobility device, Luke Sprywalker. Apparently, I'm a threat to steal!

Other works by Steve Carrier:

1958 (fiction)
What happened one year in a very small town

For Pete's Sake (fiction)
Growing up A.D.D. long before it was fashionable

A Most Unlikely Story
A summary history of the Jews

50 Ways to Love your Savior
A devotional
(Note, this is included with Geri-Active
but is also available as a stand-alone publication)

Death Rehearsal (fiction)
The Dead-reckoning of Willis Staley

Every Blamed Thing (fiction)
The Life and Times of Bergen Shantz

Geri-active
The Caleb imperative

If you think I have this figured, I don't.
I wrote this for myself because I needed it.

Pilanesberg, South Africa
This is for you older guys.
You know who you are.

Years ago in South Africa, there was a crisis with the elephant population. You would think with the world's largest land animal, humans would make a practice of keeping their distance, but typically, elephant herds and human populations behave well together. Sure, there must be a prudent respect for the beasts – but overall, the elephant has been easy to study.

It was in a game reserve called Pilanesberg that a problem was noticed. The male elephants started misbehaving. They repeatedly attacked the rhinos in the park and were an increasing threat to the park vehicles. Generally, not much bothers a mature rhino, but he is no match for an elephant. A pattern of misbehavior was forming and finally an observant zoologist pinpointed the problem. It was a shortage of mature bulls in the elephant herd, and they were sorely missed. It is a growing problem throughout Africa because of the egregious behavior of greedy men. The mature bulls had the prize tusks, and elephant tusks are a treasure.

In Pilanesberg, the young bulls, the adolescents – had no role models. In short, there was no elder bull to demonstrate restraint and order and patience. There was no mentor to usher the young bulls from adolescence to maturity. As a result, the young bulls became restive. Their hormones backfired and they tried to be sexually active before their time. They went into a heightened, aggressive condition called *musth*, usually associated with a surge in hormone levels. The young bulls were literally *in-must* of sex. The problem was, as they tried to mate, the older (but not elder) bulls beat them to the punch, and the young bulls became frustrated. Apparently, in winning the heart of a female elephant, a couple of tons makes a difference.

A sociological experiment was devised whereby some of the delinquent bulls would be moved to larger herds in reserves where there were elder bulls. In return, a couple of elder bulls were moved to Pilanesberg. I'm not sure how to move an elephant, but I don't think it's as simple as knowing a guy with an F-350. Still, it was done and soon the rebellious delinquents became respectable. They waited their turn to go into musth, and they are today on their way to becoming patriarchs themselves. The entire culture of Pilanesberg – the rangers, visitors and rhinos, returned to normal.

....

If sociologists took a lesson from the zoologists, they would find in our society a diminishing influence from our own patriarchs. Old men do not wield the same social authority as they had decades ago, and this lack of influence in family and community may contribute to the frustration of the culture. Of course, today's old men are much older than even two or three generations ago, and they tend to live further away from immediate family. Two hundred years ago, the typical man ranged within twenty miles of the place he was born. He traveled, sure, but his generational homestead was considered home. Then came the westward expansion and distances widened. By the year 1900, a second and third wave of settlers put down roots and in doing so re-established the family claim. But following World War II, America became exceedingly mobile. Air travel was practical and fast, and the freeway system was a powerful lure to millions. Suburbs appeared and families that once huddled close to each other, now had to plan a vacation just to pay a visit. Family dependence and intimacy began to decay as the telephone became the relationship instrument. In all human history, there has never been an invention so immeasurably useful – and so socially boorish. It doesn't require the caller to comb his hair or wear something decent, however it does require the caller to assume that the person he's calling has no life – except to sit and wait for the phone to ring. It is a necessary, but uncommonly rude instrument.

Today, we communicate with tiny screens and icons and emojis and have replaced the elegant hand-written letter with whatever our thumbs can text out in less than a minute. All the while, young Americans remained young – and middle-aged Americans remained middle age while older men got older and older. A hundred and twenty years ago, the life expectancy for the typical American male was forty-six years. In fairness, this low number reflects a much higher infant mortality rate than today. Still, adjusted for that, people who survived the first year of life were treated to an expectancy of fifty years or so. By 1940, the expectancy rate had jumped to sixty years, and in 1950 it had climbed to sixty-five.

Currently, it is almost eighty years – and candidly put, society doesn't know what to do with us. Moreover, we don't know what to do with ourselves. We have been marginalized, ignored, teased, pitied and praised. For society at large, we represent a problem, a delight, an embarrassment, a mystery, a financial burden and sometimes even an asset. We are stubborn, rigid, argumentative, old fashioned, corny, and almost completely out of touch with the fast lane – and yet we are the guys on whose shoulders the society was built, and we have seen it all. We are the living link between a nation that was God-fearing - but has become God-forgetting. We are like immigrants with one foot in the old world, where everything made sense – and one foot in the new where very little makes any sense at all. Still, through it all, we have experienced enough life to know how to dodge the crap before we step in it.

We are the olders, the patriarchs, curmudgeons, codgers, pensioners, grandfathers and (charitably) the senior citizens. So far as we know, throughout history, except for the grand era of the biblical patriarchs, there has never been a generation like ours.

The anthem

To some in our culture, the person sixty-five + is a caricature - almost a cartoon. Sociologists believe that since the time of the French Revolution, there has not been a single generation in the western hemisphere that did not think of itself as superior to the previous generation. This might be because the older a person gets, the more he resists change. But change happens! The earth moves under our feet and the scenery is altered whether we like it or not. Young people love it simply because it is different. Furthermore, many of them make it their mission in life to see how far they can stretch the envelope of social acceptability. By that, I mean every younger generation somehow has the notion that it is the generation that finally figures it out. With that attitude, it is no surprise that the current youth – the *arrived* generation – will test the tensile strength of established customs and standards. What we view as appropriate social behavior is constantly stretched and distorted – sometimes just for shock value, but very often as a demonstration from a generation that thinks it should be in charge. Sadly, contributing to this condition is a lack of ethical voices to pull them back into propriety.

In the meantime, senior citizens are expected to act a certain way, say certain things, suffer certain aliments and endure the shortcomings that come naturally with age as if it is written in our script. Still, we have an expectation to live up to. We are the guardians of the higher virtues; gentleness, modesty, generosity, patience and the vital, but fading necessity of mature spiritual leadership. In a time in which we are encouraged to quit work, we should be *at* work.

....

Aging is funny if you're doing a comedy routine - and our generation has become very good at advancing our own caricature. There is no lack of topics for our comedy, but most of it boils down to being forgetful, cranky, achy, tired, stubborn and surprisingly intolerant. We are pitifully out of touch with technology, social media, arts and entertainment and much of today's memes and language. We are teased by tech-savvy youth who write code and use their smart phone as a primary news source. They can do it all, except write in cursive, make change, operate a clutch, communicate in complete sentences and figure how to open a garage door when the power goes out.

It is true, we are almost laughingly forgetful (I'm sure I mentioned that). According to the caricature, we can't remember why we came into a room, or how long the cottage cheese has been on the counter. We can't recall the neighbor's name, but we remember everything about the big game in the fall of '62 – the one against Deer Park. Furthermore, what we *do* know, is that we hurt, and we can't do what we once did. We envy grandchildren who do cartwheels, and we have a grudging admiration for anyone who does a flight of stairs without a railing. Our monthly budget which used to allow twenty percent for entertainment, now takes the twenty percent and applies it to supplements.

In the caricature we talk a lot about the olden days – the good old days when a handshake made a deal. We knew the value of a dollar and we are fond of telling todays X-gen's that our first house cost $29,000 – and it was brand new. We find pleasure in this mostly because it's fun - - and it ticks them off. We brag about our own youth when there was no such thing as a bicycle helmet – and how we used to stand up on the slick vinyl upholstery on the front seat of the Dodge - and when the weather was nice – we rode in the back of a pickup. We had no laptops, DVD's, CD's, thumb drives or X Boxes, but we had friends, and we had the great, unfettered outdoors where we played until it got dark – or until someone got hurt.

We miss that, and we miss the days when we could eat whatever we want – drink coffee until nine at night – and listen to music that was understandable. We miss the simplicity of life and the general trustworthiness of society. Back then, the closest thing to a password was a locker combination. Today, we are slaves to the monster of paranoia – and we fatten-up the monster by feeding it dozens of meals a day in the form of passwords. We enter secret characters to the god of terror hoping it will be sufficient to keep our stuff safe from the predators.

Technology snuck up on us. It wasn't like the industrial revolution that plodded along for a century before it found its footing – no, technology emerged from its cocoon and almost overnight it was a juggernaut that doubled itself every eighteen months. By the mid 80's, it had blown past me without my knowledge, and ever since I have been trying to bring myself up to date. So far, I'm pleased to announce that I'm up to October 2005.

I mention technology because it is a contentious issue for many seniors. Some of us can't do much with it, and as a result, we do the most curious thing – we make a joke of it, saying things like, "Where do you put the coal?" Furthermore, the widgets, gadgets, bells and whistles are too much to comprehend. A good example is the cellular phone. I've had one for years, and recently I found out it has a camera. I didn't know this until my granddaughter pointed it out. Apparently I had been using it by accident, as there is a good shot of the inside of the glove box in our car, and two or three award-winning photos of pocket lint. We laugh and make a big deal of this, but in doing so we give the younger generation a lot of ammo. No wonder they shake their heads and offer some pity.

Finally, there are the labels we have to wear. The term *senior* is supposed to be flattering, but it conjures up a categorical description that is not at all flattering. We are tottering life units that are a pathetic shadow of our former selves. We are myopic, hard of hearing, hard of arteries, weak of bladder, stooped, hesitant, balding, wrinkled and (when we want to be) helpless people who once contributed to society, but who now spend our days organizing med-trays and looking at snapshots that featured cars with running boards. We are known for cursing the irresponsibility of the younger generation, and yet we are the ones who clog up the intersection because of an inability to recognize a green light. We might travel non-stop from Portland to Seattle with our left blinker on, but by golly, we make it home in time for supper, a game of Yahtzee and an episode of Murder She Wrote. We hang on stubbornly, as though it is our goal to live long enough to be a burden on our children.

....

Okay – the caricature was an exaggeration – but this is real. Once in a while we hear of a senior who swims a mile a day, works part time as a steeplejack then volunteers as a crossing guard. Good for him (her) – except this should not be treated as news. It should be the new normal. Swimming a mile is not the issue but living a robust and purposed life is, and this is the central issue.

If you are Christian, you are called into something. Jesus does not take His relationship with you casually. He paid dearly for you, and what He wants is for you to joyfully reciprocate. In Christ, we have identity, destiny, value and purpose, and it is inconsistent with such a glorious position to think that at some point, we've done enough, and it is time to coast to the finish line. Whether or not you are robust in body, you should be in mind and spirit. You have a wealth of wisdom. You have decades of valuable experience and many of you have the luxury of witnessing life from both sides. This is testimony in both noun and verb. You are the connection to past generations which means you have witnessed God's faithfulness and provision through good times and bad. You are a bridge to a sensibility and understanding that is sorely needed today, and it is no exaggeration that the adolescent bulls in the herd, actually need you.

1. You, me and society

The story went viral. Winston Churchill was giving the commencement address at a prominent American university, and the crowd expected profound words from the legendary Brit. He had no notes as he stood at the podium surveying the audience. Finally, he said, "Never give up. Never – ever give up." With that, he left the dais. It was reported to be a wonderful moment, except Churchill didn't really say it - at least not at a commencement ceremony. He had, however, said it for decades and he not only said it, but he tirelessly demonstrated the truth of it.

Don't give up could be the American motto. We are built on stories of perseverance, and we stand on the shoulders of a monumental past. In the language of baseball, *don't give up* means to run out the grounders. In the marathon, it is simply, to *finish*, and football players are told, *never spike the ball on the five-yard line*. We've heard the admonition all our lives, and yet when a man reaches a certain age, the message changes. Suddenly, he is advised to slow down and take it easy. It's called *retirement* – and it's great so long as the perspective is right. For starters, the man who is retiring should know why. Is he retiring *from* something, as if he's escaping a bondage, or is he retiring *into* something, as if he is graduating? Personally, I came close to spiking the ball on the five-yard line, and I am so pleased that I didn't

....

If you're sixty-five plus, and you notice that you fit the generational stereotype, it's because the culture has your number. Society likes expectations. Commerce is obsessed with categorizing and forecasting the population. For example, the medical profession knows when I can expect my hip to pulverize. The insurance profession makes a bet on how long I will live, and advertisers rely on predicted events in my life. They know when to introduce me to bone-density supplements and the benefits of psyllium husks (*a product that sounded silly until a few years ago*). They also know that if they're going to communicate with me, they need to do it before ten o'clock, and they need to do it on Matlock, or MacGyver or (shudder) Antiques Roadshow. I should be thankful for the fusillade of commercials because without them, I would be ignorant of the peril that is facing me. I am warned that I may develop a certain problem, and I am reminded of the delicacy of my aging condition. The media tells me this, and it knows that the best way to get my attention is to put a little scare in me. In other words, before they peddle their product, they peddle a little fear. That's harsh, I know, but it sells. The information we absorb is far more effective if there is an urgency attached to it, and nothing gooses urgency like a little fear.

The typical commercial pictures a guy who is in awful shape. He has memory lapses, and he avoids social encounters. He is melancholy and he doesn't seem to care how he looks or dresses. Finally, he finally consults his doctor and asks if Bynthere is right for him. The doctor smiles and pulls out a vial from his breast pocket. Apparently, the drug was exactly what the guy needed, and in the next frame he's doing yoga because Madison Avenue believes all happy people do yoga. He looks good. He hasn't a care in the world. He's much better dressed and even his wife looks younger. The drug has taken care of his sluggishness, which is good, but in doing so it *could* bring on vascular problems, hammertoe, underarm rash and any of a hundred disagreements he's never had before. Still, no worries. Big Pharma can solve the rash etc. with the right medication because they have him figured. He has been branded, classified and sorted, and while they don't know him as a patient, they know him intimately as a statistic.

I hope you know that big tech has a file on you, about a terabyte of your personal data is floating through the ether. It's called algorithms, the ultimate snoops into hour private life, and they've got you pegged. A dozen companies know what you are allergic to, what supplements you take, what movies you watch, what web sites you favor and most importantly, whether or not you are a candidate for their meds - - not the generic meds, but the new, improved meds that require a second mortgage. Sometimes I think that it annoys them to come across an old guy who has the regularity of the German rail system – and the BP count of a decathlete. Like it or not, we are an industry, a valuable contributor to the balance sheet of the medical system.

Sorry, that was harsh, and I confess to being unfair, but the truth is – I don't feel old in spite of the subtle social encouragement to take it easy and relax. Conventional media tells me *it's my time to kick back, after all I've earned it.* That's the message - and to sell it, the media spins it with regrettable terms that are supposed to make me feel good. First, we are labeled as *senior citizens*, a designation that's good for discounts, but not much more. I'm not sure of the origins of the discount idea – but if you want to get maudlin about it, you could take it to mean, "Let's give this guy a ten percent break because he won't be around very much longer." If that's the case…if the discount is nothing but a poisoned courtesy, then why not show some real compassion and bump it up to twenty-five percent.

We senior citizens are (apparently) in our golden years. Supposedly, these are the years everyone waits for – the time in life when we cash in the dividends. The talking heads don't come right out with it – but the hint is, that my time has come. I'm in the autumn of my life. My leaves are turning, and it is my season to do some yoga then quietly go away. I am urged to accept the inevitable, to hunker down for the unavoidable and welcome my decline with a blend of grace and surrender. Society is compelled (by law) to be gracious about it, but there remains a sort of macabre edge to the message.

....

Fifteen years ago, I tried to retire, and it was awful. I was supposed to rest – but rest from what? The best kind of rest is resting from work. Sure, I had projects and hobbies, but before long, I noticed something disturbing. I was missing something essential, and after some soul searching, I discovered the missing piece was dignity. There is an undeniable dignity in getting up in the morning with a purpose. It is biblical. It is inherent in our God-given identity, destiny and value, but in my retirement, I had come into agreement with a cultural stereotype that told me it was quitting time. It wasn't forced on me. The retirement gestapo didn't march me into a retirement camp and let me spend an hour a day in the exercise yard - but the underlying expectation was for me to be obedient to the system and coast to the finish line.

Surveys indicate that a growing number of men view retirement much differently than they expected. Retirement for these men became a confinement – and not a very pleasant one. It's not a prison – there are no guards or concertina wire – but there is an atrophying routine to it. We get three meals a day and plenty of time to reflect on how it all came to this. It is at this point that some men lapse into depression and begin to ask, *is this is all there is?*

You could say it started with the Jews, about thirty-five hundred years ago when this remarkable culture came up with the idea of the weekend. Well, not exactly the weekend, but at least the idea of a day off from work. They called it *shabbat*, or as we know it, Sabbath. It was one day in the week when people didn't work – or couldn't work, according to the law. As with a lot of innovations, the Jews were not only first – but first by a mile. It would be millennia before any other culture adopted the idea of a day off – let alone the notion that at a certain age, a person could actually *retire*.

For the common man during the Dark Ages, work was limited to subsistence provision. There was no industry and no commerce beyond the trading of goods for food and bare necessities. Each village was self-sufficient, typically made up by farmer, blacksmith, tanner, cooper, miller and the local church. Only the elite had time for recreation or the money to spend on it, and only the nobility and the clergy traveled. The typical peasant seldom ventured more than five miles from the place of his birth, which was, curiously, a benefit to the lord of his manor. Because life was so hard, and people so poor, raising an army or militia was an easy thing to do. The idea of marching toward adventure and riches inspired young men to leave the fields of barley to join the field of battle. In reality, being killed in battle did not shorten a man's life by that much. Life expectancy was so short, that it is said that a teen-aged girl who received a wedding shawl, would, in twenty-five years, use it as a funeral shroud.

Does this make you feel good about the present day and age? Do you feel blessed to live in these times? Obviously, since the onset of the Industrial Revolution, life expectancies rose to unprecedented levels, and it was only natural for companies – and even governments – to offer help to the worker who could no longer work. Railroad workers, firefighters and teachers were offered pensions, which of course the employees paid into – and little by little, the concept of retirement grew from an anomaly to a cultural practice.

In the early part of the 20th century, there was a notion that there was a sweet spot in a person's work history. The years of plenty for a worker were between twenty-five and forty. "A man does his best work in this span," declared the eminent physician, William Osler. At a valedictory address to the Johns Hopkins Hospital in 1905, he said, "Workers between ages forty and sixty were tolerated, but uncreative. After the age of sixty, the average worker was useless and should be put out to pasture."

Curiously, it was the Germans who popularized the idea some twenty years before. In 1881 Otto Von Bismarck introduced the concept of a state-paid pension. Slowly it caught on in America, but it took the Great Depression to push it over the top. FDR, faced with an unprecedented unemployment rate in the early 1930's, saw a way to 'take care of the elderly' and ease the unemployment problem. Older workers were holding on to their jobs, making it even more difficult for younger workers to find work at all. The idea was, of course, to get older workers to quit – by paying them to quit.

Today, we consider retirement an entitlement. Well, it would be, wouldn't it? You paid into it. The government (and or your employer) took your money and invested it for you – and that's all I'm going to say about that. Today, some eighty-five years after the

Social Security Act, the notion of retirement is intrenched in our society. We know it's coming – we anticipate it – and yet very few of us are actually prepared for the sharp reversal in our daily life. We spent decades of dedication and suddenly, getting up at six o'clock has no meaning.

Finally, this item; according to the Mental Health Foundation, retirement increases the chance of suffering from clinical depression by forty percent – and of having at least one diagnosed physical illness by sixty percent.

....

I would have retired, but for a restive spirit that said I wasn't done. It was my wake-up call, and I'm glad for it. I want God to tell me when to come in for a landing, not the Bureau of Labor & Statistics, and certainly not the *golden age* claptrap peddled by a social media that would have me live on a cruise ship and do tai-chi in the park once a week. The fullness of life is not walking on a beach at sunset – fullness is found in pursuit. It is the pursuit of the plans God has for you. Go after it, and at the end of the day, a walk on the beach is not just nice, but triumphant.

Please, this is not about being reckless. It isn't a suggestion that we take up bungie jumping to satisfy a bucket list. I'm not trying to re-invent my youth – or be cavalier with my own health and wellness. Furthermore, I'm not proposing that we should stay on the job until we drop. Instead, this is a re-examination of purpose as given to us by God, not the Social Security Administration. In short, this is knowing for sure *who* is speaking. This is about paying attention to the only One who certifiably has us figured – the One who has an adventure planned for us regardless of age. It cannot be otherwise, because *He* cannot be otherwise.

This is the scope and challenge of this little book. I can either walk in fear or faith - but not both. Only one of them can thrive and we all know that the one that grows is the one we feed. A diet of fear compromises a man. It reduces the robust, and it eventually makes a man an easy prey for the predators waiting in the tall grass. It may be that society thinks it is doing us a favor by allowing us to coast to the finish line, but the culture does not know the whole story. Society knows *who* I am, statistically – but it does not know *whose* I am. I am a child of the High King of Heaven, and He has plans for me to prosper and not to fail.

This is where we will start. Nothing happens without change – and even change cannot happen without exchange. We have to give up something to make room for new furniture, and I submit that we give up listening to a temporal society and start listening to the Source.

There's an old adage that speaks of loyalty. It says to 'dance with the one who brought you'. I like it, and I maintain we should take it one step further and fix it in our hearts to *dance with the One who bought you*. We were purchased at a mind-bending price - a price that suggests the buyer (Jesus) has an expectation of us that doesn't include resting on our laurels.

We need to have a new thought, and the best way to take on a new thought is by examining the thought that propelled you into existence in the first place. This is for old guys. If you are a young man reading this, go ahead. Before you know it, it will apply to you - and you'll wonder where the time went. In the meantime, don't let a calendar or a birthday card or the medical profession or the media tell you how you should be feeling. Ask yourself, *if I didn't know how old I am, how old would I be.*

2. Identity, destiny, value & purpose

A fish knows nothing about water. This because the fish is so dependent on the environment of water that it cannot imagine anything else, and as a result, water is simply a fact instead of a blessing. For you and me, the act of thinking is exclusively the context in which we exist, but we are different from the fish because we are sentient, and the fish is not. Still, it is impossible for us to imagine the condition of not thinking. We treat the ability to think as something ordinary, a thing that is automatically ours just for existing, but when we take it for granted, we miss out on the miracle of it.

We are incredible. An adult male is a biomass collection of some 50 trillion cells, each made up of billions of atoms. These atoms, before they are sequenced into a life-form – are inert. These are our raw materials, inert elements that God arranged in such a fashion as to provide a life unit that can consider the very concept of its maker.

We (humans) are primarily COHN, carbon, oxygen, hydrogen and nitrogen. We have trace amounts of other elements, but basically, we are COHN (*or HORC if you prefe*r). All elements in their natural state are inert, but contemporary science insists that, if properly sequenced, they will produce a biological life form. It sounds simple. All you need to do is to put a measure of each element in a blender and push the timer button for a billion years. According to the evolutionary model, this should produce a life-unit, and once that is established, it is only a matter of time, chance encounters, favorable mutations and natural selection before you and I rise to the top of the food chain.

Science has tried to manufacturer life. At one time it was believed to be easy to sequence the elements into something that was not only alive, but something that had the advanced capacity to replicate itself. That's asking a lot of a glob of inert molecules, and it's no wonder that science failed. In fact, statisticians now believe that the mathematical probability of the chance encounter of inert elements sequencing themselves into life - - is effectively zero. And yet, we are here, and I submit to you that the real miracle of life, is the emergent mind. It is breath-taking, and it should leave us asking the essential questions about ourselves, *what, where, how, when, who* and *why*. What follows is more than a primer, it is a necessary reminder of the glory of us. If you are like me, the act of aging eroded my sense of value and self-worth, and for a time I didn't feel like I was *wonderfully and fearfully made*. What follows should answer the questions of our inherent identity, destiny, value and purpose.

WHAT AM I? In this reality, I am a bipedal primate capable of intelligence, abstract reasoning, language, and emotion. I feature an erect body carriage that lets me stand upright. This leaves my arms free for handling and manipulating objects, such as tools. I am social by nature, and I appreciate beauty and aesthetics. I have a desire to understand the world around me. My body is designed to be mobile, in fact, at the most elementary level, my body is little more than transportation for the two things about me that will last, my spirit and soul. When I was born into this world, I experienced a live birth - that is, I was not planted, nor did I hatch. I have use of the opposable thumb and I am aware of my own mortality. This makes me 'sentient', and in the known universe there is nothing like me. Finally, my specie is the only creature on earth that blushes - - or needs to. This is because we inherently know right from wrong.

WHEN AM I? My life is a play in three acts, and I am currently enjoying act two. This is the act in which I get to take up space in a physical body and move around in a material world. The problem is - this act (act two) has boundaries and limitations. I am confined to experience everything in linear time, and I am a prisoner to the governing principle of cause and effect. The function of my universe depends entirely on change, or more accurately, exchange. The physical laws of nature cannot exist without exchange - - in particular the laws of motion, expansion and contraction, thermodynamics and the mysterious beauty of chemistry.

My physical universe is expanding. As it expands it cools, and as objects grow further from each other, the forces of attraction between them become weaker. Eventually, after a long time, my universe will cease to exist. It will suffer from a thing called stasis, or heat death. In other words, the thing that most people think they can depend on – nature – is a thing that will eventually cease to exist. Since the natural realm has limitations, it is inferior to the reality that will last forever. Logically, if something eventually dies, it is inferior to the thing that never dies.

So, here I am today, making my way through Act Two. Right now, I am between the bookends of eternity past and eternity future. This precise moment is the midpoint of eternity. It is exactly halfway between the existence that had no beginning and the existence that has no end. From eternity past, I have been known in the great mind of God (Ephesians 1:4). That was Act One, and for eternity future I am invited to be in the presence of God in His heaven. That will be Act Three – the final act of my story - - the act that has no final curtain.

WHERE AM I? My home is Earth. It is the third planet from the Sun and is the largest of the terrestrial planets in the Solar System in both diameter and mass. Home to millions of species including humans, Earth is the only place in the universe where life is known to exist. We orbit a spectral type, main sequence G-2 dwarf star, and during this orbit, Earth rotates on its axis 366 times. My planet has only one moon, but it is important in influencing the tides and the axial tilt. Seventy-one percent of the surface of Earth is covered with salt-water oceans. Liquid water, necessary for all known life, is not known to exist on any other planet's surface.http://en.wikipedia.org/wiki/Earth - note-6# note-6 Only three percent of the Earth water is fresh, and sixty-eight percent of that three percent is unavailable; locked up in glaciers, polar ice caps and soil. In addition, about ten percent of all fresh water is carried in great atmospheric rivers. It rides above us until conditions are right for it to fall. This is the hydrologic cycle, a miracle.

Our planet shouldn't exist – in fact, the entire universe shouldn't exist. When science considers all the necessary conditions, occurring perfectly and in order, the odds against the universe existing are so astronomical (excuse the pun) that the notion that it all "just happened" defies logic. According to a leading statistician, it would be like tossing a coin and having it come up heads ten-quintillion times in a row. This is the improbability that must be overcome just to have a universe and a host planet for you and me. The statistical probability does not include life itself, and certainly not the emergent mind.

HOW AM I? I am not an accident. I am not a product of the chance assembly of inert atoms that somehow defied the basic laws of entropy and evolved into an increasingly complex life form. I am a marvel - the zenith of physical creation and it is a very great mystery that we humans do not spend our days beholding our own miracle. The reality of our relationship with our Creator should hold us in a constant state of praise and awe.

WHO AM I? The simple and majestic answer to this is, I am a child of the High King of Heaven by whom I am extravagantly loved. There is nobody on this planet He loves more - - and nobody He loves less. His love is perfect, a quality I cannot begin to understand, but a quality for which I am eternally thankful.

WHY AM I? Of all the questions we could ask, this is the most profound. We have a primal identity, and we exist for a purpose. The chief end of man is to glorify God, but surprisingly, few Christians understand why we exist in the first place. On the surface there seems to be no real purpose for us. There is nothing we can do to make God greater, and nothing we can do to make him less. Furthermore, at creation, He knew we would be a heartache - - so why on earth did He put us on Earth? What happened before anything happened? Trying to understand the beauty of redemption without knowing our need for redemption, is like trying to make sense of the Lord of the Rings by starting with book three. That is why we have to start before the beginning, and since God is outside of time, He is before there was a before.

The story is perfect, because in the heavenlies, the reason for anything is perfect.

A right relationship with God is not something we claim at the moment of salvation, it is something we reclaim. We are not redeemed into something brand new - - we are restored into something we had in the beginning. It is not possible to be *redeemed* – if we were not at first *deemed*. In the garden, God deemed Adam and Eve to rule. They had the right to rule – first of all because God gave it to them – and secondly because they were in an intimate relationship with their Creator. Then they screwed up and man lost both relationship and rulership. We were deemed to rule and deemed to have relationship with the Father - - and we lost it. At the Cross, it was restored. We were re-deemed on both counts.

Throughout the creation narrative, God gives each event a grade. Five times after performing a work, God says *it is good,* but when He reviewed His handiwork with man, He said, *it is very good.* We got the highest marks, the summa cum laude of creation. We are the object of His affection and the crowning achievement of his work, and as far as we know, the entire universe is the backdrop scenery for the stage that is planet Earth. If this is true - - if all of it is for us, how great is His affection for man!

The Central Point: God is love, and the seminal essence of love is this; it is meant to be expressed. If a person has an asset and hoards it, it would be counted as a character defect. God has no defects. He does not hoard – and He knew that His love was nothing unless it was expressed - - but on what? This is where we come on stage. We are the necessary object of the expressed love-nature of a good God. Love that has no recipient is a heartache without a remedy. God is capable of the heartache, but for Him to be without a remedy is absurd. Simply put, without an object to love, God's boundless love would go to waste. Waste is a defect, and God has no defects.

The remedy is us. We are the cauldron into which God pours His love. We are the recipient of God's greatest asset, and it is vital to remember that we are not an experiment. God does not mess around with a thing to see if it's useful. Furthermore, love is not something God learned, or has worked to obtain…it is what He is. God is love in both noun and verb. When He spoke us into being, we became not simply the *what* of creation, we are the *why*.

We are the object of the perfect will of God, and as sentient creatures we were designed to be in relationship with Him. We pleased the great heart of God, and we also broke it. He knew it from before the beginning, and this foreknowledge is evidence of the length and breadth of perfect love. Perfect love costs dearly. If the cost was not paid, the love would be less than perfect. If the love was less than perfect, God would cease to be God. It is entirely proper for us to thank Him for simply being Himself.

Finally, this, God's love does not depend on reciprocation. The very idea that we are required to love Him back violates the nature of love. God loves us whether or not we love Him back, and His grace was not an afterthought. It existed before creation *in situ*. It was in place before we were in place. Grace was prevenient. It was waiting for Adam and Eve to step into its provision, and (thankfully) it waits for you and me.

3. Beat-up or up-beat?

I'm seventy-seven. I'd like to say I don't have a care in the world, but that would be a stretch. The thing is, I've had my share of concerns, but nothing like some stories I've heard…that is until recently. About two years ago, worry elbowed its way into my head. I've had worries before, but they were trivial anxieties - things that would be forgotten in a short time. This new worry was different, and shame on me, I gave it a foothold.

It started small – just a little fret on my seventy-fifth birthday. The years snuck up on me, and I guess I thought that getting old would take longer. Suddenly, I was running the anchor leg, and I started to dwell on it in a way man should not dwell. I fretted, and fret is a tumor. It grows into worry and if you let it, worry morphs into fear. I didn't get as far as fear, but I did experience depression, which was new to me. I wasn't gloomy; by that, I mean people were not avoiding me because I was melancholy, but it was hard to stay up-beat.

With depression came other nuisances, perhaps independent of the depression, but probably not coincidental. My sciatica got worse, then I got a wonky eye, and my leg bothered more than usual (I had polio when I was a kid and for sixty-some years I've dragged a leg around). Moreover, it seemed that everything I read was depressing. I was continuously reminded that I was zeroing in on the life expectancy figure for the American male. I tried to treat it with humor, and I even wrote a piece on it which I might put at the back of this book. Funny or not, I became more aware of my diminishing returns in the natural world, and for the first time, I realized that certain doors were slammed shut forever. I would never play second base for the Dodgers or shoot the Zambezi or even walk to the coffee shop without puffing. I wasn't maudlin about it, but it bothered me. A little depression from an up-beat guy is hardly noticeable, and those around me probably didn't know it was going on.

It's strange the things that attract attention when the mind is busy with a fret. It's as though the media had me programmed with an anxiety algorithm. Everything I saw and heard exacerbated the fret. I opened the newspaper to the obituary page, and for the first time I read it differently – taking the time to see how I measured up with those on the page. Hugo Andressen (1934 – 2021) has ten years on me. On the other hand, I've already outlived Milford Poltroon (1951 – 2021) by seven years. I know it's stupid, but I felt like I'd won something and I gave it a little fist pump until I realized I was making a contest of it. The Poltroon family would be disgusted with me.

At my age, a guy listens to a sermon on Hezekiah, and how God gave him another fourteen years. It's a good sermon, and while seniors love it, millennials wonder what it was all about. We forget that a senior thinks about age with the same frequency that a millennial thinks about bandwidth.

....

About death: Stay with me - - this isn't as bad as you might think. The way we treat death is relative. We celebrate the hundred-year-old who passes quietly in his sleep as if his years gave him enough time to enjoy life. 100 years satisfies something in us. It represents a point at which death is acceptable. This means, of course, death at any other age is tragic in varying degrees. The 100-year-old man is thought to be blessed because of the strength of the number of years. The ninety-eight-year-old is celebrated too, but here we do a curious thing. If the ninety-eight-year-old dies a natural death, we celebrate his life, but if he dies playing hockey, we treat it as somewhat tragic. There is another reason the typical ninety-eight-year-old is not greatly mourned, he has out-lived his mourners. His own kids are in retirement homes and his only living friend was off playing hockey.

Clearly, there is genuine anguish over the twenty-year-old who goes down in his prime. This sort of tragedy stirs up a sentiment that life is unfair, and to the materialist who thinks this physical existence is all there is, life is entirely unfair because (they believe) it comes to an end, forever. The Onion Newspaper recently ran a headline that announced: *World Death Rate Holds Steady at 100%.* It's true, and yet throughout the ages, people are still surprised by it.

Back to Milford Poltroon. We hear that he died and we say, "No – that can't be, I just saw him yesterday." It's as if seeing Milford yesterday put a protective shield on him…and somehow the shield failed. Eventually, when the shock of the news softens, it is time for the higher emotions, and usually the first (the culturally correct emotion) is sorrow. We show sorrow, but for whom? For Milford Poltroon or for those left behind?

The younger the person, the greater the sense of tragedy and grief – but the older the person, the more relief than grief. This is unofficial, and entirely un-scientific – but picture a graph with two vectors, the vector of grief slowly diminishing on the diagonal from upper left to lower right, and the vector of relief ascending from lower left to upper right. As grief abates with the age of the deceased, relief rises up the graph. At some point grief and relief come together. It is the intersect – the point at which people don't know if they should work up a tear or raise a toast. I'm being charitable here, but we should remember that age is not the only thing that increases the sense of relief. The guy who was a class-A, five-star jerk all his life might receive more toasts than tears, no matter how old he was when he died.

Still, there is the ultimately tragic aspect of death – and it is a death without life. For years, I served on staff at a small-town church. The town was small enough that our sanctuary was often used for funerals of people who did not profess a relationship with Jesus. The funerals were grim, sorrowful displays of despair and resentment. I cannot help but compare that scene to a very different service that celebrates the life of a saint.

The difference is night and day, a fitting picture of the Kingdom.

I have a friend named Joe who, if he outlives me, is instructed to read something at my memorial. It is my words, but not from the grave.

I'm out of here. Grieve if you must, but please, not for long. Remember, I'm the one wearing the party hat. I'm in heaven and you're not - - so neener, neener.

....

I hope you can see that I don't have a fear of death. That issue has been settled…but the act of dying is another matter. It bothers me because I want to do it gracefully – with nobility, but I don't know if I will since I've never done it before. We all want to *go easily into that good night in the fullness of our years,* and like the patriarchs of old, *be gathered to our people.* That's what we want, but who knows. Sometimes I think we're so stuck in the flesh that we're missing the sublime. We have it in our heads that death marks the end - when in fact (if you know better) you know better. Sure, it's the end of this little blip on the radar screen, but it is the very beginning of the big story in which (again, for the believer) there is nothing to fear. Zero! True, I'd like to pick and choose my own method to get to the party, and I can't think of a better example than my own dad. At ninety-three, he sat down and took a nap, and during this nap he left. He simply and beautifully left the physical realm. Way to go, Dad! That would be fine with me, that or it'd be cool to leave while playing hockey or check out during a worship service.

It's fun to think about the biblical patriarchs, and the way they treated aging. Finding the perfect card would be tough – one that says, *Lordy Lordy, look who's six hundred and forty!* Furthermore, their conversations would be strange. Two of them meet at the city gate and the first says, "Did you hear? Lamech died."

"No," says the second. "I just saw him fifty years ago - - how old?"
"Fairly young," says the first, "Not even eight hundred. Did you know him long?"

"Three, maybe four hundred years. We go way back."

....

I said I'd never died before, but in a way, I have experience with it. Years ago, I handed over my life to Jesus and let my old man die. Dying to self is the only form of surrender that culminates in victory, and when I gave Him the old behavior and attitudes and peccadillos, at that moment I became a new creation. It didn't mean I was exempt to the nature of the old man; I still have one foot in each kingdom, which means I have salvation, but not diplomatic immunity from sin. I know it, and the enemy knows it, and he really wants to take me down. He is the ultimate opportunist. He looks for a toehold, anything he can find that he can drive a wedge into and create separation. In me, over the years he's found his opportunities, and two years ago the fret began. As I said, the fret had to do with reaching three-quarters of a century, and what should have been a victory march, turned into a funeral dirge. The devil was on me like white on rice, and he stole from me. He's a thief and he should be arrested, and here's an empowering reality – as a citizen of the Kingdom, I can make a citizen's arrest.

When I say I visited the old man, I didn't mean hanging on to the sin and smudges, I mean hanging on to the memory and shame of it. There's a difference. When a bad thing happens outside of our control, it is regrettable – but when we bring it on ourselves, there is regret. This is bad. The memory of it hangs on like cigar smoke in a phone booth, and unless we air it out, it becomes the devil's playground. He loves regret. It is probably the easiest emotion to exploit because the guy with regret already feels awful. Regret becomes a sponge. It soaks up lies and negativity and us *olders* are an easy mark. This is serious stuff. If we don't deal with regret, it will morph into shame, and shame will debilitate a man. It will suffocate joy and purpose, the two virtues that set a man apart in this culture. The old guy with a joyful heart gets noticed, and once you're noticed, you have an open door to testify. You actually become a patriarch.

When you dwell on regret, you degrade your own self-esteem. You declare war on yourself. You are the one to suffer the casualty, and the devil is the one who celebrates the victory. Do this, and regret will erode your sense of destiny, cheapen your self-worth and steal your purpose. It is nothing but a highlight film of screw-ups, and when a man insists on plowing up old ground, there is only one guaranteed outcome – he will become less because of it. We do it to ourselves, and it makes us think we are unworthy. This is nothing short of an insult to the Cross of Jesus. Furthermore, the man who beats himself up over his past is doing the devil's work. Satan can't hurt God, so he goes after the creatures that God loves…you and me. Thankfully, we can do battle with him because we have both permission from the victor and a full quiver to work with.

Find out what the devil hates, then do it.

The full quiver: If it was possible to melt down the four Gospels into one great commission for the believer, it would be this: Preach the Kingdom, confess your sins and repent of them, heal the sick, destroy the works of the enemy and love your brother. Jesus said we get to destroy the works of the enemy. Note, we don't get to destroy the enemy – Jesus gets to do that later – we just destroy the works, and we do it in Jesus' name, inviting Holy Spirit and the angels to engage.

There's nothing in the world more terrifying to Satan than one man, living his life in lockstep with Jesus and doing what Jesus said to do.

Giving in is not giving up. There is power in submission, and there is also power in repenting. The trouble is, we don't do it easily. We have a lifetime of cultural training that works against surrender. It is in us. It is a part of the American male psyche, and we fight it – right up to the moment when we discover there is strength in the right kind of submission.

When we accept Jesus, we repent of our past. Once that is done, there is no need to revisit the old sin, however some feel the need to repent time after time. It's as though the first repentance didn't quite cover it, or maybe we didn't use enough church words, or perhaps God was distracted when we were trying to get his attention. Just to be safe, we repeat the repentance of sin that has already been cast away. There is no need to do this. It's like writing a mortgage check even after the house is paid for – just to make sure you actually own it.

Confession is another matter. The easiest thing to do is confess another man's sin, but when it comes to our own, it's hard. Repenting covers history – whereas confession covers current events. Other than a few seriously troubled people, it is not intuitive to voluntarily confess every little thing to each other. In the heavenlies, it's different. Confessing and repenting is actually a source of strength, and it is as uncomfortable as it is necessary. I don't think God finds pleasure in our confession, but He finds joy in our obedience to repent. It is an integral part of our relationship, and confessing never, ever moved a man further away from the lap of God. I believe repenting, for as awful as it seems, is endearing to God. The gap between the physical realm and the Kingdom of God is reduced.

Repenting never, ever moved a man further away from the lap of God.

Every day, we should renew ourselves in the Kingdom through worship, praise and repentance. We do not, however, have to renew our salvation. Salvation is ours by grace – and grace is not fickle or moody. If you try to describe the grace of God, you are guaranteed to come up short. No man can grasp or imagine the beauty and size of it. Grace is a building with no top floor.

....

What if – on the day I accepted Jesus - Father God sent the devil a telegram:

This is to inform you that the old Steve Carrier is dead - STOP – He is not yours anymore – STOP – He is mine – STOP - He is a child of the High King of Heaven and if you mess with him, and he asks for My help, you'll be in a world of hurt. STOP.

4. We could use a hero right now

Have you ever left something on the table? I don't mean fish bones or Brussel Sprouts, I mean winnings…something that could have been yours if you had been smarter, or paid better attention, or had more nerve. In real estate, the man who takes the first offer on a house, probably leaves a lot of money on the table. When he realizes this, there is regret. In poker, there is always a big difference between what a man wins – and what he could have won - - or lost. That's why they call it gambling. We don't have the luxury of peeking at the cards, no matter how much we want to.

Still, we want to know how things will turn out – and that simply is not possible, but what is possible, is to know the One who knows. This is what makes us winners. We have been bought at a price and we are told by the buyer that He has plans for us. We don't know the particulars, but we know it will be (ultimately) good because He is good. Furthermore, I don't think we are mentally equipped to know the length and breadth and scope of our potential in Him. I believe the plan God has for every man is so far beyond our comprehension, that if a man knew of it in advance, he wouldn't believe it. Nonetheless, there it is - what God has planned for you and me is mind-bending. It cannot be otherwise because God is incapable of being ordinary, and to begin to understand it, we have to have the right thought. Every morning we have a choice of eyewear for the day – world lenses or Kingdom lenses. The lenses you pick will decide your day, and after enough days, it will decide your life.

> *In the 1920's, a shoe manufacturer sent two salesmen into Bechuanaland (today's Botswana). The idea was to find out if the area was a suitable expansion market. The two came back with identical reports – but delivered with different attitudes. The first salesman was dejected. "Nobody wears shoes," he said. The second salesman, an upbeat, optimistic sort, said with excitement – "nobody wears shoes!"*

It's not new. People with attitude, make history. Of course, people with the wrong attitude also make history – so when the rubber hits the road, it's all a matter of discernment. How do you feel about a thing? Do you know who's talking? What is your relationship with Him.

…………………………..

We like our heroes, and my favorite is Caleb, the son of Jephunneh the Kenizzite. The Kenizzites were one of the nations that lived in the land of Canaan, which means Caleb was not a Jew, but he did marry into the Tribe of Judah. He eventually became so highly regarded, that he was listed alongside the descendants of Judah.

When the Children of Israel came to the border of Canaan, Moses sent out a reconnaissance team. He asked the twelve tribes to each select their champion – the toughest, most fit and most able. Moses could have said, "Give me your Navy Seal, Green Beret and Army Ranger. Give me the elite from your tribe." From the tribe of Judah, Caleb was picked, and eventually the twelve men explored the Negev and Canaan. Their mission was to make an assessment of the geographic features of the land, the strength of the population, agricultural potential and the description of the fortified cities.

For this assignment, two of them packed the right equipment. Joshua and Caleb put on Kingdom lenses (excuse the pun - but is this *knight* vision?) and what freaked out the other ten men, invigorated these two. In Canaan there were walled cities, huge fortifications, a large and strong population and giants – a lot of giants. We don't have the dialogue, but we can imagine Caleb reporting back to Moses – "This is cool - - we can take them – easy."

What did Joshua and Caleb see that the other ten men missed? Probably nothing, but what they saw, was through the lens of empowerment. They saw themselves correctly, as children of a good God who was ready to show favor to those who stepped into a right relationship with Him. The others did not have this advantage. To them, giants were giants – but to Joshua and Caleb, they were nothing but small problems on stilts. *If your thinking is small enough, everything is a giant.*

Remember, it had been only a matter of months since the Children of Israel were liberated from Egypt. The people were not accustomed to the idea of freedom, and they whined – a lot. They even pleaded with Moses, saying they were better off back in slavery. After a couple hundred years in bondage, a people group develops a slavery mentality, and while they were meant to be free, they were fearful of freedom. If we can take the ratio of Joshua and Caleb with the other ten spies, we can suppose that a strong majority of the people were settlers, and not true pioneers. They were afraid of the risk, and they were skittish about the challenge God put before them. Many of them were in such fear that they wanted to return to Egypt and spend the last miserable years of their lives in bondage. This is not only cowardice, but it is the kind of thing that propels the next generation into the same spineless worldview.

Below is a famous quote from Teddy Roosevelt, who said it – and lived it. It is called, *The Man in the Arena*.

> *It is not the critic who counts; not the man who points out how the strong man stumbles, or where the doer of deeds could have done them better. The credit belongs to the man who is actually in the arena, whose face is marred by dust and sweat and blood; who strives valiantly; who errs, who comes short again and again, because there is no effort without error and shortcoming; but who does actually strive to do the deeds; who knows great enthusiasms, the great devotions; who spends himself in a worthy cause; who at the best knows in the end the triumph of high achievement, and who at the worst, if he fails, at least fails while daring greatly, so that his place shall never be with those cold and timid souls who neither know victory nor defeat.*

This is Caleb. He came back from Canaan with vision. The vote was ten to two, but he and Joshua probably tried their best to sell it to the people. It is fair to ask why Moses didn't overrule the ten spies and go ahead with the invasion. After all, Moses wore the same

Kingdom goggles, and he was the undisputed leader of the people. To this, there are at least three reasons: (1) You cannot lead an indifferent man into war with you; (2) the people still had a bondage mentality, and it would take an entire generation to flush it out. Literally, it was necessary for the old, subservient generation to die off. Finally, (3) Moses was the leader, but he was not an autocrat.

So it was that the Children of Israel spent forty years in the wilderness, and at the end of that time, Moses was gone, as was the entire dysfunctional generation. What was left, was a new generation that was the recipient of daily blessing, protection and provision from God. For almost forty years, God fed them, demonstrated to them, and arranged for them to live in air-conditioned comfort in the desert. Finally, with only Joshua and Caleb left to remember the old days, the people were ready.

We can only imagine Caleb's frustration during the wilderness years. He was surrounded by a majority population that simply did not get it. The people were both fearful and fickle, and if our numbers are correct, eighty percent of them were wearing the wrong lenses. Their giants were indeed giants - - whereas men like Joshua and Caleb (later Samson, David and Elijah) dared to think Kingdom thoughts – and in doing so discovered they were not intimidated by anything.

These men left nothing on the table, and they knew at the end, the triumph of finishing well.

For Caleb, it is not possible to conceive of his disappointment in being turned away from the Promised Land. Back in the wilderness, facing forty years of wandering, it would have been easy for him to let frustration decide his future - - but he didn't. He had a sniff of victory, and forty years later, it was as fresh as yesterday. He literally took God at His word. He believed!

Does any of this sound familiar? Look around at society and see how many people actually *believe* something. Some do, but most are believing whatever is convenient, or politically correct or even whatever is popular at the moment. Our culture is regularly betrayed by people who claim truth, but who have only a nodding acquaintance with it. We ask the right question, *give me something I can believe in,* but we will be endlessly frustrated if we do not ask the right source.

To be sure, Caleb did not escape the notice of the younger generation. During the forty years, while his own generation died off, he didn't, and it was probably well known in the camp that Caleb's secret was obedience. No doubt he was legendary, a superhero amongst them. The powerful patriarch.

We can make a guess that Caleb himself was instrumental in turning the worldview of the youth from fearful to fearless, and in a short forty years, the tribes were ready to take on anything. Closer to home we have the undeniable demonstration of the same dynamic. World War Two – as awful as it was, created what many historians regard as America's greatest generation. Most of us had dads, neighbors or uncles who served and when they were done demonstrating, America felt like it could do anything. The unescapable influence of our heroes gave the next generation a confidence and swagger. It is commonly noted that the 1950's was America's greatest decade.

We should want to be Caleb. We should, for one day, put on Kingdom glasses and discover that our relationship with God features triumph, spiritual audacity and revelation. One day turns into tomorrow and with enough tomorrows, we have a lifetime. But it needs to be a partnership. God is not pushy. If he made decisions on your behalf, it would violate the free will he gave you. Don't misunderstand – He is involved, and He constantly works to herd you toward Himself…but in the end it must be your decision. God has plans for you right up to the amen, and whether you believe it or not, you are a hero in the waiting room. We serve an eleventh hour, wet wood burning, axe head floating, sea-parting, giant-bashing God who, by his very nature, cannot be ordinary in anything.

....

Finally, this. Caleb, in the end, fights the good fight. He follows his old spy-mate Joshua into the Promised Land, and when it came time for the land to be divided, Caleb said the most remarkable thing, "So what if I'm eighty-five - - give me the hill country. My legs are still good." He was shown favor by God and thus (almost) ends the story of Caleb. There is a little side-bar story to his life that involves his daughter.

Caleb's daughter, Aksah, was given to Othniel in marriage. Othniel, who later becomes Israel's first judge was satisfied with the land given in the dowery, but Aksah wanted more. She asks her husband to go to Caleb and ask for more, but Othniel doesn't dare approach his father-in-law. We don't know why Othniel is reluctant, but it could be that Caleb, the giant killer, became a giant to the people. He was, no doubt, legendary among the tribes. That is why Aksah breaks tradition and visits her father, boldly but respectfully, and Caleb gives her more than she could expect. Jewish culture at that time allowed women to receive gifts of jewelry or money, but never land. In a bold encounter with her famous father, Askah asked for land with wells of water and Caleb agreed. Aside from a break in tradition, there is a powerful symbolism in this story. It is clearly, a picture of the goodness of God in our requests, prayers and petitions – and it is also a profound act in the way this ancient society treated the rights of a woman.

Caleb is the proper picture of the patriarch. He is old in years and young at heart. He is feared by his enemies and revered by his nation. He is us – or at least what we could be in our tribe, clan and family.

....

So much for Caleb…but a little about Shammua, Shaphat, Igal, Palti, Gaddiel, Gaddi, Ammiel, Sethur, Nahbi and Geuel. These are the ten spies that wimped out…the ten toughest men of their individual tribes who saw giants - - and that's all they saw. They are listed in Scripture - men who had a chance to win but left a whole lot on the table because they could not see beyond their own fear. It should make us wonder what kind of men they were in their 80's…if indeed they reached their 80's.

We know there was fear in their hearts, but they were supposed to be champions, so their excuses might have been more of a plea for caution. "We're not ready," Shammua might have said, "maybe soon - - but not right now." Does this sound familiar? We all do it at some level. Certainly, I've done it, but instead of preaching on it, I'll just take a scene from my second favorite movie, Music Man. Marian (the librarian) is making excuses. She is hesitant to make a commitment, and she says, "No, please, not today - - maybe tomorrow."

Harold Hill shakes his head and says, "Oh, my dear little librarian. You pile up enough tomorrows and you'll find you've collected nothing but a lot of empty yesterdays. I don't know about you, but I'd like to make today worth remembering."

Marian sighs and says, "Oh, so would I."

Now, that's good stuff.

5. My Story

I'd like to tell you I have pedigree - that I'm a trailblazer who opened new vistas for my generation. That's what I'd like to say, but if I did, I would be a charlatan. I don't have a dynamic story with a lot of drama, in fact, what happened to me was almost pedestrian. There was nothing notable about it until I took time to reflect on it.

It was summer of 2006 and I intended to retire. I took early Social Security because I could, and for a short time, retirement lived up to its billing. I was liberated

(I thought) except for an elusive feeling that kept nagging me. It wasn't a big thing, but it was annoying, like a mosquito in a pup tent, or that little itch in the back where you can't reach without pulling something in front. We (Val and I) were getting by financially (but just barely) and I thought the nag could be satisfied with some additional income. That would scratch the itch – but as it turned out, the itch wasn't superficial – it ran to the bone. When you get a little nudge from God to change things up – and you don't want to change things up – you have what sociologists call *cognitive dissonance.* It is the mental friction you experience when you try to metabolize two contrary thoughts. That's the academic term – but I like the term my dad used. He called it *divine restlessness,* the moments when God messes with your status quo.

For me, divine restlessness was aimed at dignity and purpose – two essentials that were slipping away. There is dignity attached to getting up and going to work, and in my few months of retirement, that was lacking.

During this time, two people spoke to me, both women. Don't misunderstand, I wasn't a hermit or a misanthrope, lots of people spoke to me – but for some reason I listened to these two women. One of them had kids in my Sunday School class and she encouraged me to teach at a local homeschool co-op. She would even arrange the interview. Up to that time, my experience in teaching was with the elementary ages, and the homeschool co-op was populated by middle school and high school students – a scary prospect. Still, I decided to look into it. It would be a source of income and when you're considering work, options are always good. That is why I listened to the second voice, a friend who mentioned that she worked at Microsoft driving a shuttle, and they were desperate for drivers. If you had a pulse, you were in.

I investigated both possibilities, and in June, the school said *yes* to my idea for a curriculum, and that same week, I visited the Microsoft campus – a sprawling complex of 105 buildings populated by forty thousand scary smart techies. I was hired on the spot, and learned that I would not drive a bus, instead I would drive a Prius. There was a computer screen in the vehicle that would tell me (Shuttle # 117) to pick up at a certain building and deliver to another building. Aside from memorizing the location of 105 buildings, it couldn't be easier. Furthermore, it was only half days – and I told them that I couldn't work on Fridays because in the fall, that would be my day to teach. They bought it. I told you they were desperate.

So, I worked my little half day retirement job, sitting in my Prius, touring a gorgeous campus, talking with people from all over the world for four hours a day Monday through Thursday – and getting paid for it. I loved it – especially after I found out how to skirt the Microsoft mandate to *'never talk religion with the passenger'*. This was huge. It confirmed to me that when you take Holy Spirit with you, He will make the appointments. For the most part, I honored Microsoft's mandate and didn't bring up religion. Besides, people pay more attention to a conversation that they themselves initiate. The problem is – how do you get someone else to start the conversation that you cannot start. It was beyond me, but not Holy Spirit. This is what He does, and He is brilliant. What he did was give me a sort of a script, a teaser to a conversation, and when I followed the script, I was amazed how often it worked. My Prius was like a courtroom in which a judge cautions the parties about areas that are out-of-bounds. "However," the judge says, "If the opposition opens the door for you, you get to walk through,"

The key is Holy Spirit. Never leave home without Him. Without His help, I would have been foolish – and probably fired. As it was, I think I was useful. I prayed with people, sang with them, testified to them and generally shared whatever was available to share – and the passengers gave me permission to do it. A shuttle driver is like a hairdresser or a bartender. For some reason, you're safe - - besides, it's only a seven-minute car trip.

Here's how it worked. Most passengers engage in small talk. Most of them sit in the front seat with you, and you can tell if they are of a mood for conversation. Still, it is up to them to bring up the forbidden topic, and thankfully, the most common question they ask is the one question I needed to open the door. "Are you almost done with your shift?" they ask. In reality, they don't really care, but we are social animals and it's only proper to pretend to have an interest in another man's life – even if he is a lowly shuttle driver.

Insincere or not, it was my cue, and I learned to give it a little laugh and say, "This is my half-day retirement job, so you could say that I'm almost always almost through with my shift." It's a good line for a couple of reasons. First, it lets the passenger know that I'm conversational, or at least that I'm not a dim bulb – and second, it invites the pivotal moment. It is the moment when we look to the heavenlies to see if there is any anointing on the way. If I am to testify, I need to depend on Holy Spirit to raise up the right response, so I wait for it, and if it does not come, it was probably not anointed. However, it's great when a passenger gives me permission to testify. "Really," he says, "retired from what?"

Thank you, Lord, I say under my breath, because this is the opening of the door, and I am about to gain legal entry. I say, "I was on staff at a church" (*wait for it – wait for it*).

Just like that it comes, the testimony opportunity. "What kind of church?" he says.
It's a cool moment, a moment that makes you feel you are not alone…and so I respond. "Well, it's a Christian church that…" And so it goes.

From here it takes different directions. Sometimes the passenger clams up, but very often it engenders conversation, and over the thirteen years I worked at Microsoft, I had hundreds of encounters, which brings me to a caution and an exhilarating truth. The caution is this – in our zeal to testify, we sometimes think we have this tiny window of opportunity, and we tend to jam it up with big church words and way too much detail. It's like cramming a marshmallow into a piggy bank – you can do it, but it makes a mess of things. A revelation comes out of this. It used to bother me that passengers got out of my shuttle without any resolution other than they arrived safely at the right building – then it hit me. Holy Spirit, in his brilliance, not only choreographed my encounter with him, but He had the next encounter planned also. Who knows how many people Holy Spirit arranged to work on the guy? We don't know that part of the story, however, I am convinced that someday Jesus will invite me to watch the video, and it is then that I will become undone (again) by the brilliance of the choreography. And yes, once in a while the ultimately cool opportunity comes when I get to run the anchor lap - - the baton is slapped into my hand, and I get to take it to the tape.

A side bar story. One day I picked up a young East Indian for a short campus trip. He sat in the back, but we engaged in conversation. Soon, he asked the operative question – "are you almost done with your shift," and that question followed the script perfectly. I was loving it, and as I explained the church and its' basic tenet, and I glanced in the rear-view mirror at the guy - - and he was glowing. "Oh," he said, "If I could tell you what my Jesus did for me. I was lost in Mumbai, and my Jesus found me!" He went on non-stop all the way to his building – a young East Indian who had such good news, that he couldn't shut up about it. It was my turn to be blessed, and once in a while I get this great picture of Father God inviting the saints over to the edge of heaven to see something cool. "Watch this, "He says with a laugh, "I set this up." The joy of the Lord is my strength.

That was my Microsoft experience, an adventure that would have never happened if I hadn't paid attention to my own divine restlessness. Moreover, it would never take place were it not for the urging of a friend. As for the other part of my re-awakening – I'm still there. It is now fifteen years with high school kids, and teaching has its hooks in me so deep that I actually go into withdrawals during summer break. I love it. I've been able to mentor more than three hundred kids and they have repaid me in ways beyond value. Four times I was selected by the senior class to deliver the keynote address at graduation – and I cannot tell you the richness of the friendships and associations.

....

I'm alive, and recently I've been thinking about Caleb and the decision he made at age forty. In spite of disappointment and frustration in the wilderness, Caleb made a decision to stay at it – and for him it paid off, big time. If I can apply it to today, I wonder how the decisions I make now, at age seventy-seven will pay off at age ninety. Good things happen to old guys. My father, who at one time in my youth was as corny as Iowa, picked up a lot of wisdom when I left for college. I remember coming home after a couple of years away and talking with him. I was so proud of the wisdom he'd picked up in such a short time.

Obviously, I was the one who changed, not him. Dad was perhaps the most unchanging man I have ever known. He had a wonderful perspective on life, and I think he had an unusual grasp of linear time and how to use it. On his 90th birthday, at a celebration at church, the moderator asked him if he'd spent his whole life in Spokane. Without so much as a wink, Dad said, "Well, not yet I haven't." I have no idea how that fits into teaching, but it's too good to leave out, so I'll hand it off to you to find the genius in it.

That's my story, but not all of it. Like every other Christian guy in America, I am a work in progress, and while I've learned a lot, I still know very little. In this, is a humbling side bar. Leon Lederman, a renowned physicist, wrote a book called *The God Particle*. It is a journeyman's guide to understanding the nuclear makeup of the atom. At the end of the book, Lederman makes a confession. He said, "What we don't know about the atom is - - well – everything." I love his humility, and we should be like that with our spiritual life. We think we know the depth and majesty and beauty of our LORD, but at the same time we should be smart enough to know that we know next to nothing. Praise God for room to grow.

6. It's about time

Time flies like an arrow, whereas fruit flies like bananas. Groucho Marx

One of the perks in writing this to my age group, is that my audience remembers the same presidents. We grew up with the same music, sang from the same hymnals, and we share our own age-related trivia. We remember

Fibber McGee and Molly, wax lips, nickel phone calls and black and white televisions that, we were told, would ruin our eyes if we watched in the dark. It didn't ruin our eyes no more than swimming within an hour of a meal would kill us. That was sneaky. It was a plot started by some grownups who wanted to take a nap after lunch and didn't want to be bothered watching the kids. Remember that stuff? That was just yesterday, wasn't it?

The thing is, time is a tyrant. It is also the most valuable commodity in the world. We need it. We're desperate for it and yet we are constantly running out of it. If you could interview today's billionaires – it is my guess that the moment before they expire, they would happily forfeit their wealth in exchange for just a few more days. Most men would, billionaire or not – except of course for the man who is content. This is the guy who didn't let time sneak up on him – the guy who has the proper prospective on *his turn* on planet earth.

Time is quirky. We seldom think seriously about its passage, until something serious happens. It is then that time has our attention, and we discover that we have not treated it well. If you're seventy-five, and are average (whatever that means), you have spent 125 days of your life waiting for traffic lights to change. You've invested 85 days shaving and if you are a punctual person, you have wasted thousands of hours waiting for people to show up. I'm punctual. I like to be on time – but the problem with punctuality is this; there's nobody there to appreciate it.

With a caution to young readers – I'm going to be blunt. When the twenty-five-year-old glances at his age-gage and notices that he is down a quarter, it's not a big deal. To him, he has all the time in the world. Einstein was right – it's relative. To a six-year-old kid, the gap between July and Christmas is a lifetime, and to our twenty-fiver, the span between his age and the life expectancy is downright Methuselistic (is that a word?). However, for you and me, a look at the age-gage freaks us out because we notice the needle is pushing 'E', at least according to the Bureau of Statistics and Public Paranoia. It's true. We realize the shortage and we experience a phenomenon called *time/value equivalency*. This equivalency holds that the value of time is inversely proportional to the amount of it available. In other words, the less time available, the greater its value. It's a crazy maker because we not only have more to worry about, but we have less time in which to do it. Sadly, the time/value equivalency exacerbates fret and dread, and it does so at a time in our life when we are trying to be free of such nuisances.

What this produces, is all kinds of unhealthy thoughts that complicate an already fragile condition. For example, if you let fear and regret run unchecked in your head, there will be a feeding frenzy. Depression is sure to follow, and dysfunction is not far behind. Below is a short list of typical regrets.

- **There are so many things I wanted to accomplish, and now there's no hope for that.** *This is the spirit of failure and hopelessness. Get rid of it.*

- **I just wanted to live long enough to (1) see my granddaughter get married, (2) write the great American novel, (3) see the Mariners in the World Series.** *This is the spirit of lack. There will always be things left undone. Methuselah left things undone. Live with it.*

- **It's too soon! I'm not ready to go and I'm scared!** *This is the spirit of fear. It is an interloper from hell. If you are a Child of God, you have authority over this. Use it.*

- **I have accepted Jesus, but I'm not sure He will accept me. I really haven't done much to deserve salvation.** *This is the spirit of religion. It has nothing whatsoever to do with Jesus, and everything to do with making doubt the centerpiece of your theology. Jesus died for you. If you read 'believe in the Lord Jesus Christ, and you will be saved," and you still doubt, then you have a* *problem with the inerrancy of Scripture. Get rid of that problem and overnight the Bible makes sense -- in fact it is the only thing that will make perfect sense.*

- **I'm not done establishing my legacy. My family will suffer**. *This is the spirit of worry. Cast it out.*

What you do is this; collect the lies of the enemy and get rid of them. Make room for the change by making the exchange. Renounce the lies. Declare out loud that the enemy of grace has no authority in you. Say this: "*I am a child of the High King of Heaven, and I have been purchased by the blood of Jesus. I am His and He is mine and I claim the grace that He provided. To the enemy I say, depart from me. Take your lies and your temptations and your whisperings and shove it. I say this by the authority given to me by Jesus of Nazareth who came in the flesh.*"

....

When we are done making the exchange, the prize is truth, and it is here that we witness a curious thing. Many old people - who for much of their lives rejected the Gospel of Jesus – finally accept it as truth. Some of this might be attributed to desperation, the act of a frightened person who is covering all his bases – but let me offer this. The older we get, the less we depend on our public acceptance. In short, we make a necessary exchange, we trade out the need to be popular – for truth. While much of our culture doesn't know it yet, what it wants is readily and freely offered. We want Jesus here and forever!

This is the ultimate good news, and we should be so undone by it that we can't shut up about it. In this, we have a decided advantage. We have experience, decades of it, and experience speaks volumes. When a recruiter meets an applicant, the first question is, "what is your experience." With sixty or seventy years under our belt, we can speak to this. Our testimony doesn't need to be borrowed – it is ours alone and the gravity of it is powerful because it cannot be denied. A twenty-year-old seminary student can preach it – but we can remember it and share it.

Here's a challenge. Make a list of the times in your life when you have been given provision - - when you have been blessed - - when you have received protection - - and when God withheld the hand of the devourer. This is your testimony, and it is more powerful than any secular story you can hear because your story features the superior reality.

Scripture tells us that men will come against the faith with *'fine sounding words'* and we think that means are supposed to argue against such words, but did Jesus argue with the Romans? No, in fact the only people He got mad at were church people. Jesus was perhaps the most passive-aggressive person who ever lived; passive to the opposition and aggressive toward preaching the Kingdom. St. Augustine said, *Truth is like a lion. You don't have to defend it. Let it loose. It will defend itself.* It's true - demonstrating often works better than preaching – and it most certainly works better than trying to defend the faith by finding fault with the secular worldview. The man who sells a Buick by telling the customer how bad a Pontiac is, doesn't know his own product.

....

What we own is not only the best product on the market – it is the only conceivable story that fully satisfies our relationship with a loving God. Here's a review.

Christianity is...

- the only faith story in which God does the work, and man is simply asked to believe it.
- the only faith story that satisfactorily describes the intricate interplay between the physical and the metaphysical – with an understandable motive and logical methodology.
- the only faith story in which good works and obedience are encouraged, but not mandatory.

- the only faith story that satisfactorily explains the condition of man and provides the ultimate remedy.
- the only faith story in which God's supreme attribute of unconditional love is poured out on man.
- the only faith story that features grace as an undeserved favor _and_ provides for everlasting life with God to anyone and everyone who accepts it.
- the only faith story in which the centerpiece is the public humiliation of God.
- the only faith story that presents a detailed record of origins; a stunning account that is eerie in the way it agrees with the contemporary scientific scenario.
- the only faith story that dares to feature its heroes complete with weakness and smudges.
- the only narrative that dares to feature prophecies – all of which (to date) have been fulfilled, and none of which (to date) have failed.
- the only faith story that uses a stubborn, contrary cast of characters to play out the drama for all the world to witness. This cast (the Jews) should have died out ages ago – but didn't. It was prophesied that they would survive, and they did. Their story is a living miracle for the whole world to see.

It is the greatest story possible. Hollywood can't write stuff like this - it's too beautiful. The Cross is the singular remedy for what afflicts humankind. It is simply not possible for any sin to be greater than the covering for it, because the covering is the life-drippings of the Darling of Heaven, given willfully for you and me. Jesus did not go to the Cross against His will – He went because of His will.

7. Our future

This gets a little gritty, but it ends great.

The future you imagined when you were twenty-one had chapters written in linear time. The chapters were supposed to add up to something meaningful – a legacy perhaps, the stuff they write poems about. There's nothing wrong with that except compared to what is to come, it is tiny thinking. Our time here is a blip on the radar screen, and we (seniors) know full well how quickly it passes. And yet, there is a moment in this blip that is everything. It is the moment when a man decides where he wants to spend eternity.

The two most important days in our lives, are the day we are born and the day we figure out why. Mark Twain.

Heaven will be holy. That might sound elementary – but *holy* in its primal sense means something set apart – something so completely unlike anything else in existence, that it is futile to try to reduce it to words. We cannot describe the glory of heaven using earthbound examples, human-bound language, local colors and material dimensions. We simply have no comparisons, because for starters, heaven will not operate on the principle of exchange. It will not wear out or wind down like our universe. For you and me, Heaven will start out wonderful and go up from there. It is the place we should yearn for, and that in itself makes a mockery of the fear of death. In fact, the only conceivable reason that a Christian might fear death, is that he has not come into agreement with the assurances of God. In my experience, the three most common questions are:

- Have I done enough to make it in?
- Does heaven really exist?
- Will I even like it?

 # 1: Have I done enough to make it in? The short, simple and assuring answer is, *yes*. If you believe in the Lord Jesus Christ, you are saved. You did the sinning, that is you did the thing that separated yourself from God, and Jesus did the mending. Your part was to believe, confess and repent, but even this gets sticky because we misjudge the depth of the act of confession.

We often treat it as a criminal does. When there is no more defense – when his alibi breaks down under damning evidence, the criminal fesses up to what he has done. He owns it, and now he has to pay for it. Confessing to Jesus is different. Sure, it is admitting sin, but the purpose is this; we confess it – and repent of it and then hand it over. "Here is what I did," a man says, "and I'm sorry for it. I will turn from it. Will you take it and get rid of it?" A judge in a court of law does not do this, but Jesus does.

I learned this from personal experience - - and I still got slimed by the enemy. He has no rules, and he is incredibly cunning. In my case he suckered me into to a lie that was so slick, it didn't sound like a lie. It was almost parental – as if God was saying that He was disappointed in me because I wasn't measuring up. "I know you," the voice whispered, "you didn't go to Wednesday services because you wanted to watch baseball. What's wrong with you? Chuck and Randy and Greg were there, but you - - are you even saved?"

The lie was oily, and it messed with my faith. Evil was at play, and my head was the playground. The evidence was there - lots of guys at church have more zeal than I, and they jump at every chance to come to a prayer meeting. It was the spirit of religion picking away at my faith; a nasty spirit that turns salvation into a contest. The enemy would have us believe that God is fickle, like a sales manager goading his salesmen with salvation (or loss of salvation) as the top prize on the quota board.

While it's true that He wants the best from his people, He would never use fear as an incentive, nor would He ever be inconsistent with His promises. This is what brought me back again, a fresh understanding of God's nature and character. God is not moody. He is not given to whimsy, and He does not love me because He is supposed to. Reluctant love is nothing but a poisoned courtesy. Instead, He loves me because He *is* love. Finally, salvation is not a prize we win for edging out the other guy. If that was true, then God would be a relativist, and as a relativist, He would probably love Moses more than Joshua, David more than Moses, Paul more than David and John the Baptist more than Paul. According to this relativism, only an elite few will make it to heaven – Abraham probably, and maybe Daniel and Elijah. John will make it in for sure, he and my sister.

I hope you see where I'm going with this. Relativism means we are graded by works, which is biblical contrary. It is a spongy ideology that suggests there are no absolutes because everything is relative to everything else. Still, the relativist in our culture is applauded for being tolerant – and why not. He has the least to defend, and Satan loves it. He wants us to be relativists because in relativism there are no absolutes. God's Word is built on absolutes, so are His promises. They are *yes and amen.*

That's what I went through not long ago, and it was my fault because I listened to the whispers and failed to recognize who was talking. What follows is from the internet, so take it for what it's worth.

> A Minneapolis couple decided to go to Florida to thaw out during a particularly icy winter. They planned to stay at the same hotel where they spent their honeymoon 20 years before. Because of hectic schedules, it was difficult to coordinate their travel schedules. So, the husband left Minneapolis and flew to Florida with his wife flying down the following day. The husband checked into the hotel and, unlike years ago, there was a computer in his room, so he decided to send an email to his wife. However, he accidentally left out one character in her email address and, without noticing his error, hit "send".
>
> Meanwhile...somewhere in Houston, a widow had just returned home from her husband's funeral. He was a minister who was called home to glory after suffering a heart attack. The widow decided to check her email, expecting messages from relatives and friends. After reading the first message, she screamed and fainted. Her son

rushed into the room, found his mother. and then saw the computer screen which read:

To: my loving Wife
Subject: I have Arrived!

Dearest Love,
I know you are surprised to hear from me. They have computers here now, and you are allowed to send emails to your loved ones. I have just arrived and have been checked in. I see that everything has been prepared for your arrival tomorrow – and I look forward to seeing you then. Hope your journey is as uneventful as mine was.

P.S. It sure is hot down here!

 # 2: Does Heaven exist? In spite of the promises of Scripture, many people hold to the notion that it's just too good to be true. Heaven is wishful thinking – poetic, and beautiful fiction, but really, a supreme eternal home in the sky in which everything is good and bright and happy?

Once again, if we understand the nature, character and attributes of God, Heaven is the only conceivable reality. God is never compelled to do anything – except act in accordance to His nature…and no, it is not something He has to work at. He does not have to check

Himself to make sure He's acting like he's supposed to act. We say God is a loving God, but more to the point, He is the embodiment of love itself.

Love cares. It rewards, it shows favor, and it desires to be with the loved object. The notion that, at death, everything goes black – is counterintuitive to the nature of a loving God. It would be like Tolkien, after writing about a million words, deciding to abandon the ending. There is no victory, no ticker-tape parade, no-nothing. Could this possibly be the act of the One who had you in His mind since the foundation of time? The suggestion that awareness ends when we end, is a lie from hell. Get rid of it.

 # 3: Will I even like it? The country song said, "If heaven's not a lot like Dixie – I don't want to go." We hear things like this all the time. People say, "If there's no football in Heaven, you can have it," or "if my dog won't be there, neither will I." It is nonsense. What do you think heaven is, Alabama on a good day?"

In this world, we can't wait to buy the next great gizmo. The gadget claims there has never been anything like it, and for a month it has our attention, but a year later it's on the shelf at Goodwill. This is not heaven. It cannot be…because God is not just the latest interesting thing - He will be eternally the one who will take our breath away.

Here's where we stretch the imagination. We will be in the presence of perfection. We will be outside of time, and we will be rid of worry, fret, malice, guilt, regret and all evil forever. Furthermore, it will be impossible to have a contrary thought. Try this sometime. Sit back and see if you can go a minute without having a contrary thought. I don't mean a nasty thought, I mean a twitch of discomfort – a reminder of an unfinished chore – the prospect of something unenjoyable or an unsavory memory. Unless you are in a coma, you can't do it – not for a minute, not for a day and certainly nor for eternity.

Have you ever been on a roller coaster? If not, let's go on one. It's the world's largest, steepest, and fastest roller coaster and you are in the front seat. The coaster car clicks its way up to the top of the first dive. It seems to take forever, and the anticipation is a crazy maker. The moment it breaks over the top and begins its plunge, it has your undivided attention – in fact, I contend that it is impossible to think about anything else. That singular moment will take your breath away, and I think this is a split-second picture of Heaven. It is a moment in time that is an eternity in length – a spellbinding moment that will stun us with wonders that will hold us in a tireless state of awe. In our earth-based reality, I believe we can understand only the tiniest fragment of God's glory. It is not that we don't try, instead it is because it would kill us to see Him in

His fullness. Curiously enough, that's good news, because when we finally see Him face to face, our earthly self will have already died.

John, in trying to put a bow on his gospel, ran out of superlatives. He also ran out of paper, ink and time – and so he simply said about Jesus, *(He) did many other things as well. If every one of them were written down, I suppose that even the whole world would not have room for the books that would be written.* He was referring of course, to the life and ministry of Jesus, but it is also a glimpse of the story we are about to witness. It is a picture of Heaven.

....

Meanwhile, on this side of heaven, the Kingdom of God superimposes itself over the kingdom of man. The Kingdom of God is so vastly superior that it is beyond description. Still, once in a while we are given a picture we can use, however pale it might be to the reality of the real thing. Years ago, my wife and I made the first of two trips to Mozambique. It was my first time in East Africa, and while I knew Mozambique was a third-world nation, I had no idea it was so desperately poor. On our first day we rode through Maputo, the capital city. There was a smattering of twentieth century architecture, and an aging memory of the old colonial Portuguese culture, but for the most part, it was a city of dirt roads with chuckholes as big as duck ponds. People lined the roadside, burning out charcoal, roasting cashews, cutting hair, relieving themselves and doing whatever it took to survive in a hardscrabble existence. It was sad, until we came upon a walled compound of about five acres that was beautifully landscaped. There were a number of buildings on the grounds, but the dominant structure was elegant. It was large and uncommonly handsome and at first, I assumed it to be the presidential palace. The surroundings outside the fences were so depressing, and the compound so impressive that the comparison was unforgettable.

As we drove around the corner, I discovered what it was. There, at the main gate stood two United States Marines. It was the American embassy, a kingdom unto itself. Inside the compound, the laws of Mozambique did not apply. This five-acre parcel was a little patch of America in which American laws were in effect, and it was an awesome sight, and an even more awesome picture of heaven on earth. Later, I learned that when building a new embassy, the U.S. actually transports soil from the fifty states and scatters it around the new compound. The embassy grounds become figuratively and literally, American soil. I trust you get the picture. You are a citizen of the superior Kingdom, in spite of the third-world madness around you.

8. My Turn

Sometime around New Year's Day of 1944, my turn came. As near as I can tell, that's when I was conceived. I don't remember it, although I was there…sort of. On that day I was nothing but a biomass consisting of a few thousand cells – yet miraculously imbedded in these cells was the information that would put me together. It was an immensely complicated genetic code, and it was entirely unique. The first part of the code dealt with the fabrication of my form, and subsequent apps detailed my character, appearance and personality. The amount of information is breathtaking. If it could be printed, it would require as many pages as the entire Encyclopedia Britannica – and it is all about me!

By September of 1944, by the process of cell division known as mitosis, I had added significantly to my mass. From the initial few thousand cells in January, I now consisted of about three trillion cells, by now arranged to the pre-determined form of a human infant. Three trillion cells is a lot of luggage for a person to lug around, and finally my porter (my mother) could no longer carry me and I was released. My turn had begun, and it is significant that it started on a day that is the exact mid-point of eternity - - then again, every moment of every day is the exact mid-point of eternity.

....

That was (almost) seventy-eight years ago, and since then it has been quite a ride. I've jumped out of a perfectly good airplane, shot a hole in one and rode on top of a runaway boxcar. I had a beer with Clint Eastwood, spilled coffee on Senator Henry M. Jackson, met Bing Crosby and Arnold Palmer and drove the pace car around the track at Laguna Seca. I was elected to a public office for which I did not campaign, and today I am surrounded by a fine family, all living in the same region. When I tell this to a group of millennials, it is curious to notice what lands for them. "A runaway boxcar?!" they say. "Yes," I smile, "let me tell you about it."

I have their attention, and why not, it is my testimony, and I could not help but be me. It's my turn, and there has never been anything like me. I am singular. In personality and character, I am unlike any human that has ever lived, and yet in another way I am like every other human. I have a question that needs answering. There is an inherent question in the core of every person that wants to know 'why'. It is the one big question because it considers the biggest possible thought…God. It is not possible to ask a larger question because there is no possible answer that is larger than God.

Simply put, thinking upon God is the grandest thought possible, and I am sorry for the man who spends his life

– his one turn – ignoring the question. The materialist, the man who insists that the physical realm is all that exists, defends his position with lofty arguments that boast of arriving at the top of the food chain, a life unit free to command its own destiny. However, this viewpoint begs the conclusion that his destiny cannot occupy more than eighty years (or so) and after that, everything goes black. To overcome this liability, secularism, in all its forms, advertises itself with magnificent prose – *great swelling words of emptiness* as Peter puts it. They are pompous words that convey the small thought that our life-song is not connected to anything beyond. We are, in the material argument, limited to the five senses, the four fundamental forces and an accidental universe that produced a life-form that exists for only a moment in the physical realm – and then blows away like chaff. For the materialist, the best possible scenario is that a man will beat the life-expectancy forecast. No matter how you view it, that is tiny thinking.

Strangely, this conclusion can be tested. Give the materialist two choices:

> Option A. When you die, everything goes black. There is no consciousnesses or experience or awareness of any kind.

Option B. When you die, you are received in paradise by a loving God who has nothing but good things for you.

I believe the majority of materialists will pick option B, which means in their hearts, they hope their material worldview is wrong.

The secular argument tries to make our brief existence a meaningful one, but in the end, it too is a tiny thought. As a consolation, the secularist tries to claim a connection to the cycle of life, as if this whimsy provides hope and destiny. It is a desperate notion that suggests, if he's lucky, he gets another go at it. As for me, I have considered my story and I know that I am intimately attached to a good God who has good things for me. It's my turn, and that is what I'm going to do with it.

....

Never underestimate your part in the story. Unlike secular stories, the screenplay written in heaven has no small parts. You are not an extra or an afterthought and God does not give you a bit-part in the background just to keep you occupied. Granted, our role might seem small, but that's because our view of the story is limited. We have a street view of the parade of life, whereas God, the writer of the script, takes in the entire parade, and I believe it would stun us to know the size of the role we are intended to play. Take a minute and write down the most radical idea you've ever had. I don't mean forming your own grunge band and going on the stadium tour, I mean a ministry idea…a business idea…an investment idea. Why did you dismiss it? What was its' source? Was it the One who said *I have plans for you…plans for you to prosper and not to fail?*

As for me, I think often of those days driving shuttle at Microsoft. I have no idea how many people I talked with about the faith, and I'm afraid to know how many I could have talked with but didn't. Still, at some point in the exact middle of eternity, Jesus will sit me down and put in the DVD so that I can see the whole parade. I will get to see the parade, the little assignments and how Holy Spirit took a moment of obedience and made something come of it. To my reckoning, it is the 4 x 100 relay at the Olympics. I run my hundred and slap the baton into the hands of a teammate. The thing is, we seldom know the teammate – but Holy Spirit does. This is the view of the parade from the blimp.

Billy's story: We've all heard stories of the great men of the faith, and how they got their names on the marquee. For example, Billy Graham might not have amounted to anything if he hadn't gone to a tent meeting to hear Mordecai Ham. That night in the tent, Graham was moved by the Spirit to go into the ministry, and we could leave the story at that, except we would miss the first three legs of the relay – the legs that got the baton to Billy.

Years before the tent meeting, Ham was inspired by Billy Sunday, who was evangelized by a man named Wilber Chapman. Years earlier, Chapman life was changed by a sermon from Frederick Meyer, who had been tutored by Dwight L. Moody. Moody, before he was an evangelist, was a simple shoe salesman who one day sold a pair of shoes to Edward Kimble. After the encounter at the shoe store, while in prayer, Kimble listened to Holy Spirit who told him to go back to the store and share the Gospel with Moody. He did. What might have seemed like a little bit-part in a big production turned out to be legendary.

My guess is, most Christians could trace their own dance back through the generations – and in doing so, marvel at the way they were led into the faith.

My story: For me, it was my Aunt Minnie. I am writing this today because of a woman of faith who, in 1946, stopped by my parents' house every Sunday morning to take myself and my sister Vonnie to Sunday School. That's all she did. So far as I know, she never lectured or preached or otherwise shared the Gospel with my folks, however the gravity of her actions got ahold of my father and mother. They came under conviction (not condemnation) and they started taking us to church themselves. That was it. Their visit to church had been tenderized by the prayer and obedience of a woman of faith. In a matter of weeks, my folks accepted Jesus and never turned back.

That was seventy-five years ago, and from their faith and steadfast commitment, the generational harvest has been significant. We can thank Aunt Minnie, and she in turn can thank someone in her own ancestry who is long forgotten by everyone except God. The choreography is stunning, and yet it is not up to us to understand the dance itself, just the steps. For that, it sometimes takes nerve, but remember what Wayne Gretzky said, "You will miss 100% of the shots you don't take."

Larry's story: One day, Jesus and his guys sailed to a pagan land on the eastern shore of the Sea of Galilee. It was a strange trip because it seems they went to talk with just one guy…and he was nuts. Along the way, Jesus ticked off the locals and single handedly messed up their economy - but the mission was accomplished.

The guy isn't named, so we'll call him Larry, and he was demon possessed. Even his issues had issues, but when he met Jesus, he knew who He was…and so did the demons. Jesus cast out the demons and the next time we see Larry, he was bathed and clothed and was in his right mind. We know he was in his right mind because he begged Jesus to take him on as a disciple, but Jesus told him to stay and tell the people what happened.

We don't know if Larry argued the point, but we can make the assumption that he didn't. The One who just healed him, said he was ready. If Jesus had the power to deliver him from demon possession, He had the authority to set his mind straight and put his tongue to work. Larry was humbled, and while he might have tried to convince Jesus that he wasn't ready for it – that he needed a couple of years of training – Jesus assured him that he was ready. "Just tell the people what happened to you," Jesus said.

Remember Paul Harvey? He'd tell a story, then provide the insight to it. Luckily, for our narrative, Scripture lets us discover what happened a few months later when Jesus went to the Decapolis the second time. On His first trip, Larry was the only one He ministered to, but on the second trip, four thousand people showed up. These were the people who were furious with Jesus for damaging their economy (the pigs) – the people who four months earlier, chased Jesus away. Yet, here they are, gathered in a great crowd to welcome Him. What did Larry do? Was he the first missionary? We don't know, but we do know that something happened to Larry that was so wonderful that he couldn't shut up about it. It is the perfect picture of the power of testimony. "Let me tell you what happened to me," you say to a man. When you push out a testimony with a good heart, Holy Spirit makes sure it lands in a soft spot. And that's the rest of the story.

....

We have come full cycle - - actually, we have come two full cycles since the time of Joshua and Caleb. The two of them endured the wilderness and finally stood on the banks of the Promised Land. They had stories, and experience and knew firsthand, both disappointment and triumph. We are like them. We seniors can preach with authority like no other age group. We've been witness to it, and our message should be the battle cry of the ecclesia, to return to the days when the presence of God was the selling point, not the pretense of man. We saw the triumph of the middle part of the twentieth century, and we also lived through the wilderness decline of the last forty years. The experiment with the user friendly, cupcake church didn't allow for facing giants or taking the land, but we have Caleb's among us. That said, here is my prophecy: *Old men are going to make more waves in their time left, then they ever did in their time spent. These will be Kingdom waves – waves that will last – waves that will lap against the shores of eternity.*

9. Weird…on purpose

If you are a professing Christian, but still have questions about the inerrancy of Scripture, I'm sorry. You are probably conflicted by your own uncertainty because there is little you can say or believe for sure.

Imagine treating the one narrative you can trust – with uncertainty? It puts a man in an awful place somewhere between charity and contempt, and it is here that the idea of the *fear of God* becomes frightening. To the unbeliever, the *fear of God* is terrifying because it represents judgment, but to the believer, the word *fear* becomes a quality. It is the unmistakable understanding of the nature, character and attributes of a good God who cannot help but desire good things for His kids. This exalted definition of *fear* replaces being *scared*, with being *awestruck*. It is the fear that overrules all other fears, and the man who steps into a right relationship with God, immediately rids himself of a thousand temporal concerns. He dismisses anxiety. He no longer worries about provision. He is free of depression, foreboding and fret and he no longer distresses over death itself. Throughout the Bible we are told to fear not; in fact, the command appears 365 times. Jesus said it and his followers demonstrated it. Coming into agreement with the right kind of fear will turn a man of any age from acting like a victim, to becoming a conqueror.

....

If this was a traditional secular self-help book, this is where the how-to bullet points would be. They would suggest that – if you follow the steps, you will be happier, thinner, less irritable, smarter, self-satisfied and free of the embarrassment of any of a hundred complaints common to the geriatric. I like bullet points, and I'd like to offer some, but I can't. Instead, this is about the way Holy Spirit works in a man, and it would be fatuous for me to try to consolidate the work of the Spirit down to a few bullet points. He is beyond genius in the way He customizes His work with every man. Remember, if we were identical, God could have stopped with Adam.

The upshot is this - - what Holy Spirit has for you is between the two of you. I don't have it figured and I believe on a temporal level, nobody has it figured. That's why we have Holy Spirit who (when asked) lets us in on an individually crafted plan – a pre-ordained blueprint for you to *prosper and not to fail*. If you think for a moment that Jeremiah penned those words with only money and status in mind, think again. The word *prosper* includes mental, emotional, spiritual and physical wholeness.

That said, I've boiled it down to two bullet points.

- The Bible is the inerrant word of God. It is true – all of it. If something rubs you wrong, ask Holy Spirit about it. You have coffee with Him every day anyway.
- If you don't have coffee with Him – start. He knows you better than you do…and he even knows the secrets you keep from yourself. It is my belief that when we get used to enjoying the counsel of Holy Spirit, we make the leap from believing in God – to *believing* God.

It is fitting that we pay one more visit to Father Abraham. For the first ninety-nine years of his life, he and Sarai moved around, prospered and built a name for themselves. Life was good except for one thing, Sarai was barren, and they had no heir. Sometime in his ninety-ninth year, God visited Abram again. It was the fifth time it had happened, which is meaningful.

God told him a number of times that he would have descendants, but Abram must have wondered if God's word was inerrant – or just poetic. On this, the fifth encounter, something landed with Abram and as a validation, God changed Abram's name to Abraham, inserting into the name the letter *heh*, which is forever imprinted in Abraham and his descendants. *Heh* (in Hebrew) means *life, by the grace of God.* It was not an incidental name change, that is, it was not something that simply altered the way he was addressed by others.

Instead, it was the kind of change God wants to make in the hearts of every man. For Abraham, it completely transformed him, and it was following this change of heart that Abraham received the desire of his heart – a son. God is complete in all He does. It is equally profound that Sarai experienced the same metamorphosis. She became Sarah.

This cathartic moment in his life marked the change from a full temporal life – to that of a life of fullness for the Kingdom of God. In the passage in Genesis, it says that Abram fell on his face before God. He put his face in the dust in humility and obedience, and he rose in awe. He had the *fear of God* – the right and proper fear that changes lives and generations. Technically, the name Abraham means father of multitudes, and this is precisely what the church needs today…men who will properly father multitudes.

We need men who believe all of it. This current secular generation claims to be certain of its own humanism – but it is no different than every generation for the last nineteen centuries. The secularists try to diminish Scripture for good reason – it gets in the way of their humanism. Men, for nearly two thousand years, have tried and failed to frame Scripture as a collection of myth and lore – as nothing more than fiction that is dressed up with poetry. Every generation has tried to reduce the Word of God, and none have succeeded. It is the inerrant Word of God. It is genius in its message, continuity, theme and delivery. It is weird because it cannot help but be. It is the act of the supernatural superimposing Himself on humankind. What's not weird about that?!

The mistaken notion that Scripture is a collection of nice stories that may or may not be literal - - is a lie from hell. When we hear an accusation like that, we should ask the question, *"who could possibly be pleased by such a lack of conviction?* It is not God, and that is for certain. It is also certain that the day a man confesses to the supremacy and inerrancy of the Word of God – is the day he can get rid of a thousand uncertainties in his life. It is the Abraham moment – the moment when he not only *believed in* God, but he *believed* God.

10. Our Spirit, Soul & Body

There's bad news and good news. The bad news you already know, the flesh diminishes. It does this naturally according to the law of entropy, and there's nothing we can do about it. But with God, who deals with eternal matters, there is always good news. Our Creator installed in us an eerie essence that is intended to operate with the flesh, but independent of the flesh.

We are in three parts, spirit, soul and body. When we decay, it's the flesh that is doing the decaying. The spirit is another matter. It is the mysterious impartation from God to man that does not wither because it is tethered to the Ageless One. Our spirit is intended to be the mentor for the soul. Our spirit is a docent, a guide through the things the soul is not equipped to comprehend. Collectively, body and soul are referred to as the flesh. The flesh was formed out of clay, a previously created thing. That is why man (the body) returns to the clay (dust to dust). The soul and spirit are different. They were infused in us by the breath of God. We have in us an echo of the Ancient of Days.

The body is that part of us that interacts with physical properties and the laws of the universe. Because the body is subject to the physical laws, it is the part of us that is temporary. It is little more than transportation for the spirit and soul, but it is the part of us that we seem to cherish above all. In reality, if we could view the whole of our everlasting existence, the time spent in the body is the smallest blip on the radar screen. It is next to nothing, and yet it is the housing for our experience. It is the vehicle that makes our soul and spirit portable.

Our soul is the part of us that contains mind, will, emotions and material memory. The soul is everlasting. It survives the body, and the sentient soul of humankind is the wonder of creation. It is our awareness – and our memory. While our body is the vehicle, our soul is the instrument through which we understand and contemplate the physical realm - but the soul alone is insufficient to contemplate the spiritual realm.

Because the soul was granted free-will, it is vulnerable to corruption. It is the part of us that needs saving. When Adam and Eve exercised their free will to sin, the soul became contaminated. Jesus saves our soul. When we come into a right relationship with God, it is our soul that is rescued and redeemed.

Our spirit: If there is a contentious topic regarding the essence of man, it is the nature of our spirit. It has been poorly defined, frequently argued and quite often ignored as a vital part of our make-up. And yet, there are one-hundred-ninety mentions of our spirit in the Bible. These are mentions using lower-case 's' and should never be confused with the upper-case 'S' which references Holy Spirit. The meaning of the word *spirit* in Scripture denotes a thing in us. It is *not* intended to describe a human characteristic or attribute (as in school spirit), instead, most of the one-hundred-ninety mentions of spirit are nouns, not adjectives. In other words, the Bible speaks (often) about a *thing* in us - - an animated part that is able to receive divine influence.

This part of us is not incidental to the whole, it is essential. Both Paul and James gave *spirit* the priority, saying, *"May God himself, the God of peace, sanctify you through and through. May your whole spirit, soul and body be kept blameless at the coming of our Lord Jesus Christ."*

I believe that, if properly interpreted, our spirit is our highest, deepest, and most noble part. By the help of the spirit, our soul can lay hold on things incomprehensible, invisible, and eternal. The spirit perceives faster and deeper than the soul can contemplate. In short, our spirit thinks, while the soul often messes things up by thinking about thinking. In Scripture, spirit refers to that essence that helps us make a quick understanding of a thing…a breeze of wisdom across the rational soul that aids the mental disposition. In other words, it is the still-small voice that clarifies a thing – a separator that allows the cream of an idea to rise to the top. It is no accident that the words *spirit* and *truth* are often linked together.

....

For us seniors, what follows is exceedingly good news. As our bodies diminish – and for some, our minds along with the body - our spirit remains intact. It is active, ready and anxious to be put into use. This is not a frivolous idea motivated by wishful thinking, instead, it is biblical. There are dozens of examples in Scripture of people who put soul aside for a moment and experienced life in the spirit. They turned their spirit lose to interact with Holy Spirit and the results were remarkable. He intended us to have the highest distinctive value and destiny of all creation, regardless of our age, and yet (here is the mystery) He will not impose Himself on us without our invitation. He does not violate our free-will, but He does enable us with a reality that can heighten our quality of reason and intellect. Every Christian should recognize the amazing, but mostly ignored truth that within him is a life essence called spirit. It is the wonderfully mysterious image-embryo of God, infused in man at creation.

You are spirit, soul and body. Figure it out. Sit quietly and ask Holy Spirit to make Himself known. If you do this with a right heart, He will open the bandwidth and begin to speak into your spirit. It is His job. He works tirelessly to point us to Jesus, and when we properly see Jesus, we will never again see ourselves as deteriorating, worn-out old men. This is exceedingly good news. Our spirit is young. It is fresh as Eden, and as refreshed as Pentecost.

For you and me (us older's) I truly believe that we are intended to be stronger than ever in the spirit. I also believe that what God has in store for us will so completely overshadow the complaints of the flesh – that we will become like calves leaping from the stall. God is not just asking us to get a grip on the reality of our age and condition, he is asking us to celebrate it – and find extravagant blessings in it. He has intentions for all our seasons – and none of His intentions include the idea of simply putting a good face on it and slogging our way through a tough time.

We have the dignity of being called children of God, and the highest expression of this dignity is to be in communion with God. Jesus showed us how it was done. We are already regarded as his children, but when we enter into communion, we can claim sonship. We know Him as Elohim, the Creator of the meadow. In this name He is sovereign. At the same time, we get to know him as Abba (Daddy), and in this name we have the delight of playing with Him in the meadow. We have sonship, and it changes everything because when we identify with the superior reality, the things of earth grow strangely dim. The frets and anxieties of this lesser realm diminish as we concentrate on our God. If you are like me, you have come from son – to father – to grandfather – to patriarch. If you do it right, you have the ultimate blessing of going back to sonship. The difference this second time around is that the new sonship is not only superior, but also eternal.

....

I confess this is where I need training. I'm 77 years old and I find myself becoming a son again, and the sonship I am invited into is light years beyond my previous experience as a son. While that first experience was wonderful, it was an allegiance to a man – a good man to be sure, but still a man. My dad could do anything, fix anything, calm my fears about anything and teach me anything. My regard for him was probably as elevated as any relationship with mortal man, and it is strange to think that he, my father, was just the tiniest hint of my heavenly father.

Later, I learned that my father could not do everything. He was not invincible, nor was he immune to error. He was mortal – a fine mortal, but still a mortal with feet of clay. Just writing that line, brings a pain to my heart because Asahel Carrier was an extraordinarily good man…far better than most if not the very best of them all. He was the man who called me son – and the man who I discovered later, knew how to be a son. He was perhaps the most Christ-like man I have ever known, and it has taken me most of my life to understand what made him so good. He did what Jesus did - - he loved the Father.

Here's what to do. Begin with the fundamental realization that you couldn't even think this thought without Him – and end with the stunning truth that He sees you as righteous because in you He sees the

Darling of Heaven who redeemed you. He is not blind to your sins, but instead he looks beyond your sin and sees a greater dignity – He sees a son. Moreover, He waits until we are ready to come into this reality. He did for me.

There was a time in my life when I had it all – I thought. I was in my late 20's and had climbed to the position of sales promotion director for a major west coast brewery. It was exciting and exotic. The company made me go to the Reno Air Races, the Baja 500, the NASCAR Riverside 400, the Bing Crosby Pro-Am and the Laguna Seca USAC Championships. I had a big salary, a big head and an even bigger expense account and by the reckoning of most young men, I had the best job on the west coast. That was then – before I died to self. Today, I can truthfully tell you that my worst days right now are infinitely better than by best days back then.

What happened to me was about as subtle as a tsunami. Position, money, notoriety and glamour had failed, and I was a mess in need of a redeemer. What I needed was somebody who loved me more than I loved myself, and to this there is only one conceivable answer. It is Jesus, the lover of my soul. He didn't promise that it would be easy, but He did say it would be good. I was hoping He would tell me that He would keep the wolf from the door – but we live in a fallen world where bad things still happen to good people. If you think the world will be easy on you because you're a good guy, you'll also think that the bull won't charge you because you're a vegetarian.

11. The wake-up call and the test drive

They're not just stories, they're demonstrations. In a nutshell, the Old Testament exists to show us our need for redemption, and there is no shortage of need. Even the good guys screwed up and needed a wake-up call. We read these stories, and we wag a finger toward David or Jacob or Jonah because we're indignant. They're supposed to be our heroes, and we're embarrassed by them. If you've done this, you're missing the point. The point is, everyone's faith wobbles once in a while and that's the bad news. Sure, we are children of the High King, but that does not mean we have diplomatic immunity from sin. The good news is, we are covered by grace.

Don't misunderstand this. Grace is not a *get out of jail* card, nor is it something that a good father offers because he feels compelled to do it. You would be surprised at the number of people who contend that God owes us something because He gave us the free will that got us into jail in the first place. That's nonsense. Grace is not compensation for damage –

instead, it is love at work. It is part and parcel of the perfect provision flowing from a perfect God who gave us perfect promises.

God's promises are all *yes and amen*. They are issued and kept perfectly, but in our reality, we don't really know what this means because we have almost ruined the word *promise*. Certainly, in the material realm, we have the word *promise* – but human experience has taught us to mistrust the very intent of the word. First, we dishonor the word by making it conditional - - and to protect ourselves, we look for loopholes to escape both the promise and the conditions in the promise. If it was possible to keep score of the promises made by man – and the percent of them broken - we might ask why it is that we have a word that carries such a lofty ideal. It is said that a promise is like a baby – easy to make but hard to deliver. To demonstrate this, we need look no further than politics. During an election year, we are the audience for the *national promise competition,* and from this comes a sad truth; we should perhaps vote for the man who promises the least, because in the end, he will be the least disappointing. I promise.

Clearly, Calvin Coolidge was not one of our great presidents – and yet of all the presidents, it was Coolidge who broke the fewest promises. He did it by not talking. Silent Cal said very little during his term, and it was said that *"Coolidge done nothing...but he done it well."*

The upshot is this, most of our training is to be suspicious of a promise. Even as kids we temper our oaths with deceit. The rule on the playground was, if you had your fingers crossed, you were somehow exempt from holding a promise. From childhood we were learning the art of the empty promise - - seven-year-olds perfecting the art of suspicion and deception.

Our cavalier use of the word *promise* has made it difficult to metabolize God's use of the word. His word *promise* means what it says, without codicils or exit strategies. It is so wonderful that it's hard to believe – and yet we often forget His promises. Since we are trapped in an egocentric predicament, the physical realm commands the majority of our time and experience. If we don't guard our spiritual priorities, our attention gets sucked into the gravity of the flesh. It happened to Moses, who, one day in the wilderness, forgot who he was dealing with. By this time in his life, he'd seen it all. He saw the burning bush, watched the ten plagues, walked on a dry path across the bottom of the sea and was witness to the stunning deliverance from bondage of an entire nation. After that, you'd think he'd learned the lesson...but there's no counting on the vagaries of the human condition. One scary day,

Moses forgot the promises and instead, let disbelief become the centerpiece of his theology.

In the wilderness, the people were demanding meat, and God told Moses to tell them that in the morning they would have meat. On hearing this, for some reason, Moses' faith hit the wall. What God had just told him - was too much and he blew a gasket. In his mind it was impossible, and he told God in so many words that His (God's) promise was a bit of a stretch. Moses shouldn't have thought it – and he certainly should not have said it because an exchange like that usually does not go well. Who did Moses think he was dealing with…a sort-of god who had his fingers crossed?

Moses was eighty-something when he led the people into the wilderness, and he should have known that God can do anything, with any man of any age, anywhere. Still, on this occasion, instead of partnering with God, Moses took off his Kingdom lenses and put on the lenses of the world. In doing so he forgot the burning bush, forgot Egypt and even forgot the parting of the sea…but he would never forget the moment that God got scary. In reading this narrative, I sometimes think I can actually hear God's voice. It was the voice of a patient, loving, long suffering parent who finally *had it up to here* with an insolent teen. God thundered, *"Has my arm been shortened?"*

With that, Moses got his wake-up call. He remembered who he was serving, and he remembered his history with God. If we can read between the verses, we would probably see a man so completely freaked out – and so embarrassed by his disbelief that he might have wished he was dead. He didn't die. In fact, he went on for another forty years – but following the 'chewing out' there was no hesitation. He learned his lesson and he went out to the people and told them (all 1.5 million of them) to expect meat in the morning. He might have added, "I don't know how it will happen – but God said it would happen…and take it from me, don't question Him on it."

In the morning there was meat.

…………………

The wake-up call: Moses got one. David got one. Jonah got one and certainly Saul (Paul) got one. There is hardly a biblical character who didn't receive at some point, a necessary wake up call. Travel forward a few millennia, and it's our turn. Granted, God might not get scary like he did with Moses, but He will be no less effective. In truth, it is Holy Spirit who does the work, and He is surprisingly gentle – and sneaky. It is Holy Spirit who is the mosquito in the pup tent – that annoying restlessness we experience when we need a jump-start. In this, I am convinced that Holy Spirit is out to wake up the patriarchs of the west – us older's who thought retirement actually meant retiring. Many of us have swooned – lulled to sleep by a patronizing society that thinks that our greatest contribution, is to stay out of the game.

Is that the way Scripture reads? Does it comply with any of the promises of God? Can you conceive of any possible scenario in which God tells a righteous man to ride the bench? Certainly, he tells men that there is a season for everything, including rest - - but we must not confuse *rest* with shutting down. We are meant for more – always more, and God is daring you to take Him up on it. One of the primary promises of Scripture is this; "I will never leave you nor forsake you." On this, there is no expiration date, no codicil, and no senior discount. Furthermore, to think that God has run out of things for us to do – is an insult to His character. He has work for us, meaningful work - - probably groundbreaking, fore-runner work. He is not in the business of giving us busy work just to patronize some old guys. That's as bad as the condescending participation award they hand out to a kid just for showing up at a soccer game. No! what He has is Kingdom work; meaningful service that will benefit our own descendants. That's what He has, and He dares us to take Him up on it. In Malachi, there is the Clint Eastwood passage. It has to do with first fruits, but the narrative applies to everything God has in store for us. God says, "*Try me in this – and see if I will not open up the windows of heaven and pour out for you such blessing – that there will not be room enough to receive it."* God is saying, in a loving way, *"Go ahead, make my day!"*

Is Holy Spirit testing you? Do you notice that mosquito in your own pup tent? Know this for sure, He sees the beginning from the end and He regards you greater than you regard yourself. He is the author and finisher of your faith – and He wants you to finish well.

………………………..

What good is a wake-up call if there's nothing to get up for?

The test drive: The truth of a thing does little good until it is applied. It's like dreaming about a new car. You see the ads, know the specs, study the car in the showroom and talk with others who rave about its' performance - - but nothing happens until you take it out for a test drive. Seriously, we need to move beyond feeling good about a promise from God – and actually take the promise out on the highway and open it up.

It happened to me. I believe in missions, and for a long time I was active at the church level raising funds, chairing the missions committee, and being a cheerleader for those with enough righteous chutzpa to do something about it. Then Holy Spirit sneaked up on me. He orchestrated a simple and safe event, and when it was over, I felt dangerous. It wasn't long after the event, that my wife and I accepted an invitation to work in Mozambique. It was a wake-up call, one of several in my life, and the blessing was so profound that we couldn't wait to go again. The second time we were both in our sixties, and while we did some good work in Africa, Holy Spirit did some major work in me.

We should be forever progressing in our faith. As a youth, my faith was dominated by fear and duty. So far as I knew at that time, Christianity was all about sin-management and hell-avoidance. Later I discovered a personal relationship with Jesus, and thankfulness overran fear. Then came a period when I was captivated by theology…not captivated by God, mind you…but the study of Him. It's commendable to study the nature, character and attributes of God, and we should know what we can about Him, but not at the expense of *knowing* Him. I caught myself in this. I had become an amateur theologian*, and I used what I knew to show off. This is wrong on a lot of levels. You ever come across a theology that magnifies man, flee from it. It is a theology that will hold you captive in the kingdom of man. It is your own personal Babylon, and you need to be set free.

> * We are all amateur theologians. When you consider it, a professional theologian is a person who works hard to become less ignorant about God

than the average man. In truth, what we don't know about God is – almost everything.

After my release from captivity, I was finally open to Holy Spirit and the beautiful truth that the Spirit that raised Jesus from the grave is in me. It is something that makes me enterprising and just a little daring. This makes me vulnerable to failure, but so what! If we are in a right relationship with God, we might experience failings – but we will never fail. God never – ever permits anything done in His name to go to waste. If I had been spiritually awake when I was a teen, I would have seen that demonstrated in my own house.

My father was a very average man – in almost every way – except for his faith and constancy – and who knows how many lives he affected for the Kingdom. Many of the people he influenced were young men, and into his nineties, my father hosted a weekly prayer meeting at his house for young men. At his memorial, they spoke of the remarkable impact this old guy had on their lives. Dad played the patriarch for another generation that needed to see what constancy and righteousness looked like. This is for you and me. It is our chance as a patriarch to bless the generations and do what Jacob did.

....

It's time to reclaim our bully pulpit. Of all age groups, ours is the one that speaks from the weight of experience simply because of the number of miles on our odometer. The young man speaks impulsively of entitlement and recognition. The early middle-aged man considers status, social position and security; and the late middle-aged man speaks of accomplishment and refinement. We older's, on the other hand, have the decided advantage of speaking through experience – and we have reached an age that is relatively free from peer pressure. We have the advantage of having lived life experiences that are not borrowed. They are our stories which makes them our testimony. Please, never underestimate the power of testimony. In the right place and at the right time, your story is nuclear.

For starters, we know from real life what makes sense, and you would think that it would be logical for the younger generations to ask us what we believe and why we believe it. After all, there is a phenomenon the younger generations should be investigate. It is this; the older a person gets, the more conservative he is likely to be. This is not a trend particular to our own generation – it is particular to every generation, and the size and consistency of this phenomenon is remarkable. Please, I am not linking conservatism with Christianity exclusively, however the worldview is similar. It is simply a fact that younger people are disproportionally liberal, and as they age, they drift steadily to the right, becoming just as disproportionally, conservative. With a nod to the fairness doctrine, there is some shift among seniors from conservative to liberal – but on balance, the overwhelming numbers go the other way.

There are those of us who remember the halcyon days of our youth. We sang the Age of Aquarius *(Harmony and understanding, sympathy and trust abounding, no more falsehoods or derisions, golden living dreams of visions, mystic crystal revelation and the mind's true liberation).* We wanted to go to San Francisco and wear flowers in our hair because finally there was *a new generation with a new explanation - - people in motion.*

Yes, the times they were a-changing, and now, fifty years later, they are a-changing back. So, what is it in the experience of years that persuades a man of a particular age to abandon the mentality of the sixties and return to the God of his youth? Is age itself a wake-up call or is it the persistence of truth knocking at his door that finally gets his attention. If it is a return to truth, you would think it would be a narrative of great interest to the culture at large. The problem is…the culture at large won't hear it from main-line media, except perhaps in a scornful fashion. This leaves it up to you and me, after all, it is our story – which means it is our testimony, and this presents a powerful opportunity. It represents a huge segment of seniors who sampled both the liberal and conservative lifestyles, and after a life-long evaluation, chose the conservative path. You would think that with our growing numbers, seniors would have a stronger voice in our culture, but we don't – at least not yet. We could blame the cultural attitude that we are irrelevant…but that's a cop out. Instead, the problem is us, and our attraction to the *do-nothing* retirement. We were told we were loveable and eccentric and forgetful and fragile – and we bought it. It felt good. It was both patronizing and comforting and it took us off the hook for taking any actual risks. The problem was, it put much of our generation to sleep, and now we find ourselves in a stupor of inactivity. Retirement should not mean an escape from work. Granted, it can represent an escape from drudgery, and there is nothing wrong with that - - but it is entirely possible that in these freedom years, we have an opportunity to do our most meaningful work.

We seniors have an audience if we dare to address it. We are patriarchs who are shaking off the institutional sedative of retirement because for many it is not healthy, it has not proved satisfying, and it certainly is not biblical. I believe we, collectively, are a glacier on the move. We know right from wrong by experience, and there is power in that testimony.

…………………………………………………..

In the kingdom of man, we are patriarchs – yes – but we never give up our real identity in the Kingdom of God. In that superior reality, we are sons, and we do not outgrow sonship. We are held by the Ancient One – our timeless God who sees in us a spirit that old age cannot diminish. When we step into this truth and ask God to restore what we have given away, we just might see ourselves as the Father sees us – as one of His kids. There is not one of God's kids who were intended to be average. God is not ordinary, and we are in His image, which means we have what it takes to be irresistible. This is when we become like calves, leaping from the stall. Praise God.

God will never ask you to do anything without also equipping you to succeed. Just remember the promises – and claim them for yourself. Try Him in this. Take his promises out for a test drive. If the promise is from God – you will be better because of it, and you will discover that His arm has not been shortened. God never does anything without doing everything, and to all seniors, I firmly believe we have in front of us the most productive season of our lives. We represent the return of the patriarch, and like the mature bull elephants of Pilanesberg, we can help to bring instruction and sensibility to the generations, and unspeakable satisfaction to ourselves.

That does it. We've gained altitude and you are now free to move about the Kingdom.

INTERMISSION

One thing I ask from the LORD, this only do I seek: that I may dwell in the house of the LORD all the days of my life, to gaze on the beauty of the LORD and to seek him in his temple. For in the day of trouble he will keep me safe in his dwelling; he will hide me in the shelter of his sacred tent and set me high upon a rock.

These are the words of David, and while he makes a great role model, he still comes up short. So does Caleb, Moses, Daniel and even Paul. They all come up short because Jesus set the standard. He is our demonstrator. He is the one who points us to the Father, and since He is the only personage of the Trinity who ever got a blister, or a bruise or who blushed or knew suffering first-hand – He is the one we should try to model.

Anything you think you know about God – that you cannot see in the personage of Jesus, is bad theology. Jesus is your model. He endured the cross – not *against* His will, but *because* of His will. When we concentrate on Jesus, we come to know the Father. Holy Spirit makes sure of that. Remember, the Father points us to Holy Spirit – Holy Spirit points us to Jesus and Jesus points us to the Father. They are never in disagreement. The trinity never does anything by a 2-1 vote.

....

Part of my personal wake-up call came two years ago when Valerie and I accepted a challenge. Families in our church were encouraged to celebrate communion in their homes every day from Easter to Pentecost – a period of fifty days. We agreed to do it, and the effect was remarkable. We saw Jesus reflecting in facets we hadn't seen before.

Midway through the fifty days, I heard an old classic on the radio. The song was familiar, a catchy but dispiriting thing called *Fifty Ways to Leave Your Lover*.

Just slip out the back, Jack - Make a new plan, Stan
No need to be coy, Roy - Just get yourself free
Hop on the bus, Gus - Don't need to discuss much
Just drop off the key, Lee - And get yourself free.

There was something about the song that was trying to get my attention, and in a moment of quiet, it came to me. If we had kept track during our communion meditation, we probably experienced at least fifty ways to love our Savior.

That's what follows - a celebration of Jesus.

My encouragement is for you to read one a day. Invite Holy Spirit into your reading – and as your docent, He will show you the majesty of your Savior / Redeemer. The 50 ways are only a fraction of his beauty. Jesus is a building with no top floor.

50 ways
to love your Savior

Day one
JESUS, THE ONE BEFORE THE BEGINNING

We say we create, but that's not what we do. The best we can do is to fashion a thing from pre-existing materials and concepts and arrange them into something that we think is new. In our imagination, we conceive marvelous things, but in the end, all we have done is borrow from that which already exists. The root of it is this, everything after Creation, is a contrivance of that which had been created in the first place. There is nothing new under the sun.

All things were made through Him (Jesus) and without Him nothing was made that was made.

In the beginning it was Jesus who made physical existence a reality. It was so magnificent that we cannot conceive the genius of it. He brought into existence a universe that takes up space (a new idea). It was a universe that contained particle (another a new idea). The new universe was in motion (a new idea) and it depended on cause and effect (still another new idea). Finally, this new physical realm operated on the exchange of heat (another new idea), and none of it would have happened if He hadn't introduced the idea of linear time.

Here, we can correctly use the word *create*, which means to bring something into existence that didn't exist before.

Now comes the reason for it all. In a non-descript corner of a medium size galaxy, He caused there to be a blue-green planet that would be home to an extraordinary creature. This creature would be special to the heart of the Creator because the creature would be sentient. It would have the ability to comprehend its surroundings and be aware of its own mortality. Most of all, it would be the only life-unit that could ponder its own existence and rejoice in its Creator. The creature is you and me, and the rest of the universe is an extravagance for our benefit – a thing He made like a theater backdrop for us to enjoy. We look at our universe and wonder why it's so big, while Jesus sees it as a gift to us. It is His trinket.

When I consider your heavens, the work of your fingers, the moon and the stars which you have set in place, what is mankind that you are mindful of them, human beings that you care for them? From Psalm 8

Day two
JESUS, THE CASTING DIRECTOR

It wasn't the way Hollywood would have done it. if the movie moguls were put in charge of telling the greatest story ever told, they would have surrounded the hero with the twelve most clever, handsome, brightest and gifted men available, a sort of sanctified version of the Dirty Dozen.

Thankfully, Jesus was His own casting director, and He hand-selected a curious assortment of men. For starters, there was the most despised character in the region, a worm of a man who, though a Jew, served the Romans as a tax collector. Then, Jesus chose at least three men who were fishermen, but who were apparently not that good at fishing. He took a thief who would later betray him, and then he recruited a loafer who He found lazing under a tree. If that's not enough, He hand selected a guy who had a problem with the basic concept of faith. Finally, there was the presumed leader – a ready-fire-aim sort of man who talked big when things were going well, but who slinked away from the action when it got dicey.

Of all the men who were available in ancient Judea, these were the men He called, and the thinking man should ask *why*? The answer is sublime. Jesus, at the very beginning of His ministry, did something that would set his pattern - He demonstrated. He was showing the world the mind-bending power and influence a man can possess if he first possesses the heart of the King, and almost to a man, their stories are glorious.

Eventually, this rag-tag troop of men, full of hope, joy and the Holy Spirit, changed the world. These were work-a-day guys who were lifted out of the ordinary and into the extraordinary, and two-thousand years later, we know their names and their stories.

The good news in this story is twofold. Jesus selected some unremarkable men who went out and birthed the church. If it stopped there, it would be astonishing, but it doesn't stop there. His demonstrations are for all time. He calls every man to Him, and it is simply not possible that what He has for you and me – is mediocre.

Day three
JESUS, THE HERO

No other religion dares to present its hero as one who willfully surrenders His kingship to become a servant. Welcome to Christianity. Jesus reduced Himself from His position as the Darling of Heaven, to a mortal who knew pain, joy, anger, loneliness, love and even anguish. He knew compassion, heartbreak and death, but through it all He did not know sin. Still, at the Cross, He became the very transport for sin. He took it on him, and He wore it and carried it into death so that He could deposit it forever where it was belonged, in the pit of hell.

He is a hero who never hurt a man but has saved hundreds of millions of them. He never conquered a city, but He regained dominion over earth. He never married, but his Bride is without number. He had power but He never flaunted it, and while He had all authority in all things – He deferred to the Father for everything.

It is the greatest story possible. The superhero marches into battle with the supervillain, and the hero insists on dying?! What? Hollywood can't write stuff like that - it's too beautiful. The Cross was, and still is, the singular remedy for what afflicted humankind, and it is simply not possible for any sin to be greater than the covering for it, because the covering is the blood of the Last Lamb. It is the life-drippings of the Darling of Heaven, given willfully for you and me.

The Christian faith is the only faith in which the supernatural does the suffering and the believer is simply asked to receive it. It is the only religion that features the public humiliation of God. It is the only faith story in which good-works and obedience are encouraged, but it is not necessary for a disciple to clean up his act before he seeks the presence of God. Finally, it is the only faith story that satisfactorily explains the condition of man and offers the impeccable remedy. Finally, it is the only faith story that dares to position the Savior / Redeemer as a servant.

Day four
JESUS, THE CHOREOGRAPHER

"He made all the nations, that they should inhabit the whole earth, and He marked out their appointed times in history and the boundaries of their lands."
from Acts 17:26.

Beautiful Jesus, the maker of the universe, came at precisely the appointed time. The nations of earth did not know it, but for generations they had been dancing to the steps of the Choreographer. The great empires, each in their turn, prepared the way and put in place the necessary conditions for the coming of the Anointed One. The Persian Empire – in an unusual act of benevolence, released the Jews to go back and make ready the City of David. A hundred years later, the Greek Empire took its turn, giving the western world a cultural package that included the language that would be common throughout the realm. Another two hundred years passed, and Rome established law, ensured safety and built roads. At no previous time in history could good news travel in a single language, as fast and as safely as it could in the appointed time.

The empires didn't know they were playing a part, but God did. He also knew seventeen hundred years before Rome, that the focus of the story would take place in the best conceivable geographic location. Judea is the confluence of three continents, Asia, Europe and Africa. It is known as the King's Highway, the principal thoroughfare of civilization, and it passes through the land of the Abrahamic Covenant. Abraham left the sleepy little town of Ur of the Chaldeans and relocated to the runway of O'Hare Airport. The covenant that God established with Abraham has no end date, no conditions or codicils. A covenant is always in place, and all of God's promises are *yes and amen.*

For nearly four-thousand years, while civilizations rose and fell, the Abrahamic Covenant remained in effect. We should stand in awe of the fact that, on May 14, 1948, the flag of the sovereign state of Israel flew again over Jerusalem. He is a promise-keeping God. He is the great choreographer of the dance of the nations.

"...neither death, nor life, nor angels, nor principalities, nor powers, nor things present, nor things to come...shall be able to separate us from the love of God, which is in Christ Jesus our Lord."
Romans 8: 38, 39

Day five
JESUS, THE FAMOUS ONE

Did any famous people come from your high school? I didn't think so. It's hard to imagine any of my high school classmates becoming a Supreme Court Justice, and it's not for a lack of intelligence, it's just that they went to my school. It's the bane of familiarity. I know too much about them. I know who had trouble with the truth and I know the classmate who raised a welt snapping me with a towel in the locker room. It's hard to make the leap from towel snapping to Constitutional Law.

It is not new. Historically, a prophet is not honored in his hometown. Jesus was viewed with suspicion in Nazareth because He was so familiar. According to the locals, nobody that good or wise could come from next door. For the people of Nazareth to receive him as the Messiah, they would have to contend with the improbability that – of all the villages in the world, of all the ages – why here and now? It's a mind-bender and to the locals there must be another explanation.

But before we dismiss the Nazarenes, we need to confess that we still do it. People push Him away because the story might get in the way of comfort and popularity. Some try to domesticate Him, to turn Him into something less - something semi-divine perhaps. They dismiss him because they would rather have a god who intercedes in a time of trouble, but otherwise does not interfere. Still others are so beaten down by the enemy that the *good news* is simply too good, and they are not worthy to be a part of it.

Objections to the faith always have their roots in an inferior perception. We say, *it is too strange, and too improbable to have happened;* but in the same breath our society readily accepts the massive improbability of the chance assembly of inert molecules into the wonder of sentient life. Take your choice, the materialist gamble of one chance in trillions, or the wager of one chance in two on the existence of Creator God. Either He exists, or He doesn't.

For those who experience Jesus, that wager becomes one chance in one. He is the Son, the image of the invisible God, the firstborn over all creation. He is Jesus, the Famous One.

Day six
JESUS, THE CONSTITUTION

Nineteen of the forty parables that Jesus told had to do with the Kingdom. It is a superior reality that has its own government and constitution, and if it had a preamble, it would read as this:

PREAMBLE: We, the Triune God of the Universe, in order to form a perfect union, establish eternal justice, ensure tranquility, and provide for the common blessing and welfare of all people, do establish this Kingdom for all men - for all time.

BILL OF RIGHT: From Philippians 4:8: "Finally, brothers and sisters, whatever is true, whatever is noble, whatever is right, whatever is pure, whatever is lovely, whatever is admirable - if anything is excellent or praiseworthy - think about such things."

We appreciate our United States Constitution because it strives to be mostly fair to the most people. America is a republic, which means it features the rule of law. Nobody is (supposedly) above the law, and when reduced down to the essentials, we need laws because we need ways to correct people who wouldn't otherwise do the right thing. Jesus fulfilled the law, but notice, He did not abolish the law. His purpose was threefold; to establish the Word, to embody the Word and to accomplish all that was written in the Word. He is the culmination of the law.

All the while, Jesus talked openly about the Kingdom where the throne of God is established in righteousness and justice. It is the perfect realm with Jesus on the throne, and we will want it no other way.

To our thinking, the Kingdom is bizarre beyond all comparison. It is entirely contrary to our physical realm and its beauty is beyond our imagination. Our inability to grasp the fullness of the Kingdom is our loss, but it might also be our protection. If we could see the full measure of its beauty, it would probably kill us. With that, it is fitting that when we finally see the fullness of the story, we will have already died – yet never to die again.

Day seven
JESUS, THE PREVENIENT ONE

Col 1:14, He (Jesus) is before all things, and in Him all things hold together.

Throughout the creation narrative, God gives each event a grade. Four times after performing a work, He says *It is good,* but when He reviewed His handiwork with man, He said, *it is very good.* We got the highest marks, the summa cum laude of creation. We are the object of His affection and the crowning achievement of his work.

God is love, and the seminal essence of love is - that it is intended to be expressed. If a person has an asset and hoards it, it would be counted as a character defect. God has no defects. He does not hoard – and He knew that His love was nothing unless it was expressed - - but on what? On you and me, the object of the expressed love of a good God. We are not simply the *what* of creation, we are the *why*. We pleased the great heart of God, and we also broke it. He knew it from the beginning, and it begs the ultimate question - why on earth did he do it?

Creation was not an experiment. God does not noddle around with a thing to see if it's useful. We are a part of the perfect will of God. As sentient creatures we were designed to be in relationship with Him. There is nothing like us in the known universe, a creature that exists as God's necessary expression of love.

God's love does not depend on reciprocation. He loves whether or not we love Him back. His grace was not an afterthought. It was in place before man was in place. Grace was prevenient. It was available and waiting for Adam and Eve to step into its provision, and (thankfully) it waits for me. Thank you, Jesus that the remedy for my sin existed before the foundation of time. I thank you that you knew me before there was a *me*. Praise you Jesus, the One who loved me - even though you knew it would cost you everything. You knew my defects, my rebellion and my pride, and you still went ahead with Creation. What kind of love is this?

Day eight
JESUS, THE ALTOGETHER

A father tosses his little boy into the air and catches him. The boy loves it, and says, *do it again, Daddy,* and the father does. There is no fear, no apprehension, no chance in the world that the daddy will fail. The child does not operate out of fear, he operates out of trust. Trust gained is the foundation for faith, or the other way around – faith tested is trust gained.

Jesus says, I will never leave you or forsake you. Come to me and I will give you rest. He means it. He is good. If He had a defect, He would cease to be God. He is good without any conceivable qualifications to His goodness, that is why it is nonsense to question his motives. While we might not understand His methods, we know they are good, and they work together for good. The only question is, how do we empty ourselves of fear, anxiety, doubt and selfish motives? Try this, be a kid again. Let Him throw you into the air. Trust Him, and you will surely say, *do it again, Daddy.*

It's not easy at first because the temptation of the flesh is to mitigate anything that claims to be everything. In the flesh, we have no reference point to something perfect, and we are suspicious of anything that claims to be absolute. That is why some men try to domesticate

God. They water down Scripture simply because they haven't experienced its reality in their lives. It is, in their thinking, too good to be true.

A person is missing the point if he thinks that Jesus is somehow less than everything. There is absolutely nothing provisional about Jesus. He is superlative. He is sufficient, unlimited, unquestionable and without limits. He is the perfect Lamb, which qualified Him to be the Last Lamb.

Just for fun, see if you can find the mistake in the following verses:

- I am one of the ways, the truth and the life. Hardly anyone comes to the Father except through me.
- Behold, seventy-five percent of all things work together for good.
- Come to Me you who are weary and heavy laden, and I will see what I can do.
- For God so loved some of us, that he gave his only son….
- Much of scripture is God-breathed…and some of it is useful…
- Cast half your cares on Him, and He will see what He can do.

Day nine
JESUS, LOVER OF THE FATHER

*For God so loved the world...For Jesus
so loved the Father.*

Can we safely say that Jesus first love was the world? Can we say that His over-reaching passion was to save the fallen world? Perhaps. Since deep antiquity, the Hebrew (Jew) was told to, *love the Lord your God with all your heart, soul mind and strength.* We read that as the first commandment, but essentially, it is the second commandment. According to the magnificent Shema, the first commandment is to listen. "Hear O Israel."

Leap forward a few millennia, and we read the story of Jesus taking his guys up a mountain. There, Jesus was transfigured in a spectacle that made the disciples fall to their faces. "This is my beloved Son, in whom I am well pleased. Hear Him!" This was the voice from the heavens. Notice it says *in whom* and not *with whom.* There is something mysteriously profound in that. The point is, the Father is transfiguring Himself to the Son. If you read it right, you can almost hear Him. God is grabbing us by the lapels and is shaking us saying, *Listen to Him! This is Me talking!*

God is love and it is inconceivable that He expends a greater or lesser love on any person. But remember, Jesus of Nazareth was in the flesh. He was the Son of man, subject to all things common to man except sin. He had a first love, and it was the Father. This is the echo of the first commandment.

What do we take from this? Everything! He is our model, the one who demonstrated how to love the Father. It was His love of the Father that made him pursue the Cross – because the Cross was the necessary act that satisfied the Father's wrath against sin. Our first commandment is to love God. Jesus obeyed it. He pledged himself to the first commandment, which means (sorry to break this to you) we are His second love. One of the great purposes of Jesus in the flesh – was to demonstrate the love of the Father. Jesus is *always* modeling righteousness.

Day ten
JESUS, THE STORYTELLER

Since deep antiquity, men have been drawn to the storyteller. Storytellers (the good ones) attract a crowd, and clearly, the best story is one that resonates personally with the listener. By mid-Matthew, Jesus had collected His disciples, and without doubt, around the evening campfire, Jesus told stories to His 'guys'. The word spread, and suddenly it was not a private audience anymore. Jesus had taken his message from the camp site to the stadium tour. Crowds were so great that more than once He used a hillside as an amphitheater, and one time used a boat while His audience lined the shore.

He knew his audience, and He used stories of everyday life to illustrate Kingdom truth. He is not only *in* everyday life – he *is* everyday life. "I will open my mouth with parables," He said, "I will utter things kept secret from the foundations of the world."

He was connecting the dots between the obvious visual illustrations, and the superior reality of the Kingdom of God. He made sense, and the crowds kept coming. He was irresistible, because in addition to the stories, He healed. In the healing and in the stories, He was setting up His message. Imagine, facing five thousand people and taking the time to heal everyone who asked, then when He was done, He would look over the grateful and enthusiastic crowd and say, "Now that I have your attention, let me tell you about the Kingdom."

He was doing something else too, He was demonstrating to you and me. He is the model and we are the regional distributors of His product. "Watch me," He said, "You will do what you see me doing." He is Christ, the Anointed One, and we are Christian, the little anointed ones - but make no mistake about it, the source of the anointing is exactly the same – the Holy Spirit. With a source like that, we can't help but become irresistible.

Day eleven
JESUS, THE FIRST

No, it's not like Charles the First, or Henry the eighth, Jesus was the alpha. He was the first in everything of the Kingdom.

- He is the first-born over all creation.
- He is the One who was before all things.
- He was the first in baptism.
- He was the first to be a worthy, permanent abiding place for the Holy Spirit.
- He is the first in resurrection, and the first to abide entirely in the Spirit.
- He is the first to fully understand, transport and demonstrate the abundance of the Father.
- He was the first and only to offer a sacrifice that was sufficient to satisfy the Father's wrath against sin.
- He was the first to demonstrate the Kingdom to mankind, and He was the first to model the anointing that comes with a right relationship with the Father.
- He was the first and only to empty Himself of His divine nature.
- He was the first to conquer death.
- He was the first to conquer sin.

- He was the first in ascension.
- He was first to demonstrate the Father's unconditional love – even to the unlovely.
- He was the first to rely entirely on the Holy Spirit for wisdom, revelation, comfort, power and provision.
- He was the first to be fully equipped to carry out the original command to *subdue the earth*.
- He was the first to take back dominion from the enemy – and hand it back to man.
- He was the first to fully represent the Kingdom.
- He was the first – and only sacrifice to be sufficient.

He was the first in all these things – and He was also the last.

- He was the last Word.
- He was the last thing the devil wanted to see.
- And, praise God, He was the last Lamb.

Day twelve
JESUS, THE CHRIST

Jesus is His name, and *Christ* is His title. Christ means the Anointed One.

Christianity is...
- the only faith story in which God does the work, and man is simply asked to believe it.
- the only faith story that satisfactorily describes the interaction between the physical and the metaphysical – with a believable and logical methodology.
- the only religion that features as its central event, a public humiliation of God.
- the only faith story in which good-works and obedience are not a drudgery - but are instead a blessing.
- the only faith story that suitably explains the condition of man and provides the ultimate remedy.
- the only faith story in which God's supreme attribute of unconditional love is poured out on man.
- the only faith story that features grace as an undeserved favor <u>*and*</u> provides for everlasting life with God to anyone and everyone who accepts it.
- the only faith story that presents a detailed account of origins; a stunning account that is eerie in the way it agrees with the contemporary scientific scenario.
- the only faith story that dares to feature its heroes complete with weakness, smudges and feet of clay.

- the only narrative that dares to feature prophecies – all of which (to date) have been fulfilled, and none of which (to date) have failed.
- the only faith story that uses a stubborn, contrary cast of characters to play out the drama for all the world to witness. This cast (the Jews) should have died out centuries ago - but didn't. It was prophesied that they would survive. They did.

We are followers of Christ, and as Christians, we are the little anointed ones. We have in us the same power that raised Jesus from the dead, and we are meant to use that power to advance the Kingdom. None of this we do ourselves. We do it by calling on His name & trusting the Holy Spirit to enable us by grace to perform the work.

Day thirteen
JESUS, THE SECOND ADAM

How would a person go about defending himself to God, without the covering of the Cross? Is it even remotely conceivable that a man could argue his own righteousness? We don't know who he is, but at some point in human history, there was the second-best man who ever lived. Jesus of course, laps the field, but for a moment, try to imagine this second-best man standing before the Father. He knows he has tried to live a righteous life, but he has his smudges. Some of them he can remember and confess, but most of them are fleeting indiscretions.

The Father knows it. He knows the crevices and secret closets of the mind, and the man knows that He knows. The second-best man also knows he is without defense. Why would the Father invite him into His heaven? Why would the Father contaminate His perfect heaven with a man who is infected with sin, even if it is not much sin? There is none righteous, no not one.

There is an old and tired argument that people make. "I'll go to heaven," they say, "I'm a good person." The basis for this is frivolous because it depends on everything being relative. A man measures his *goodness* by putting himself on a scale, but only if he is sure that the man on the other side of the scale is a degenerate. "I never killed anyone," the man says. Meanwhile, the man on the other side, who *had* killed a man, wants to be weighed against a serial killer. When stretched to the extreme, Hitler could claim relative goodness because he only killed twenty million, whereas Stalin killed forty million.

Jesus was the second Adam. The first Adam was created perfect, and his assignment was to subdue the earth – which probably meant to destroy the works of the enemy. Adam (the first) failed, but Adam (the second) didn't. Jesus, the Son of Man and God incarnate, became our remedy. When He was finished, when He rose victorious from the grave, He redeemed us. In the Garden of Eden, we were deemed to rule, then we were doomed – and finally, redeemed.

With Christ in us, the works of the enemy – no longer works.

Day fourteen
JESUS, THE HOST

An invitation comes in the mail. It's for a party, a celebration and if you aren't busy, you might go…on the other hand, it might interfere with something else you want to do. You're conflicted because the invitation says RSVP. What do you do?

If you throw it away, or ignore the invite and tuck it away with other things, you cannot at the last minute, dress up and go to the party. If, on the other hand you respond, saying *no, it's not for me, thank you very much but I have other things I'd rather do* - - then that's it. The party is out of the question. Still, in the Kingdom, God is constantly sending out invitations, and for some people, their first RSVP is uttered with their last breath.

In the making of mankind, God inserted a wonderful – awful thing called free will. Our will is entirely ours, and that is why, when we get the invitation – it's up to us to say yes or no. Jesus is at the door – but there is another personage of the Trinity at work, the secret service branch who speaks into our spirit. This is wonderfully weird because it is intended to be. We are spirit, soul and body, and our spirit is the receiver into which the Holy Spirit transmits.

In Scripture, there are 190 mentions of man's spirit. Spirit is a noun, not an adjective, and it is the premier essence of our existence. James got it right, we are spirit, soul and body – in that order.

Our spirit is the agent that is able to connect with the Holy Spirit, and it is through this connection that the Holy Spirit calls us. While Jesus waits for the RSVP, and while the Father prepares a place for us, the Holy Spirit does His work. He invites, sometimes subtly, with a divine restlessness, and sometimes it is as subtle as a train wreck.

To the soul, God gave the ability to gain knowledge, but to the spirit, he gave wisdom. There is a huge difference. Knowledge is knowing that a tomato is a fruit. Wisdom is knowing that you don't put a tomato in a fruit salad.

Day fifteen
JESUS, THE RANSOM

In Europe during the Middle Ages, ransom became an integral part of warfare. An important knight, especially nobility or royalty, was worth a significant sum of money if he was captured, but worth nothing if he was killed. For this reason, the practice of ransom contributed to the development of heraldry. It was a way in which a nobleman or a knight could advertise his identity. By implication, it established their worth, and the greater the worth, the more the ransom value.

The value of a person can be determined by the price that is paid to redeem him. If you dare to think you are unworthy, then have another thought. The notion of unworthiness is contrary to the reason for our existence. Unworthiness makes for an awful worldview and spongy theology, besides, it is an insult to the Cross of Jesus.

Still, there is an amazing paradox in this. We say we are unworthy, and in the temporal realm as sinners, we are unworthy, but in the Kingdom where everything is upside down, we have the highest value. Remember, when we step into a right relationship with God by claiming the blood of Jesus, we become a new creation. We didn't get an overhaul, we became new.

On the night Jesus was betrayed, He underwent a series of illegal trials. All though the ordeal, He was taunted, rebuked, spat upon, scourged and beaten. In this time, He answered only one question. When asked if He was the king of the Jews, He said, "It is as you say."

We can assume that they were baiting him. He was being tried because He claimed to be king of the Jews – which was in their eyes a blasphemous thing. Indeed, it would have been blasphemous if it was not true. Throughout the night, Jesus offered no defense, and in the flesh it is fair to ask *why;* however in the spirit, the reason is manifestly obvious. He didn't defend Himself because He wasn't representing Himself - He was representing me, and I am without excuse. He is the Ransom, and I am the one being set free.

My heraldry in the Kingdom is in the color and design of nobility. My value is that of a child of the High King.

Day sixteen
JESUS, MASTER OF TIME

He's demonstrating again, and when we take a closer look at Him, we see Him ministering on multiple levels. The screenplay for the following performance was written by Luke. In it, Jesus is putting on a show for the people of ancient Judea…and for you and me.

Dramatis Personae
Jesus, as Himself
Jarius, synagogue ruler
Crowd
Disciples
Sick daughter
Professional mourners
Sick woman

Jesus is in a crowd when an important man named Jarius interrupts Him. His daughter is dying, and he begs Jesus to come immediately. Jesus agrees and they try to leave the crowd, but a woman catches Jesus' attention. They talk and if we read between the lines, we might see an anxious and exasperated Jarius. His daughter is dying, and the one person who could save her is sidetracked by a sick woman. But is Jarius exasperated? Does he respond to the tyranny of the urgent, or did he believe Jesus was beyond that? Did

Jarius have knowledge that the Son of Man, the one who created the concept of linear time, was in command of time?

Apparently, Jarius believed at a lofty level, because even after hearing the devastating news that his daughter had died, he did not abandon his mission. Jesus was about to do something miraculous. He was about to wade through the mourners and those who ridiculed Him – but notice - He did not ridicule those who scorned Him. He did not say, *I'll show you*, instead he honored Jarius and his wife by allowing them to watch the superior reality at work. In the space of a couple of hours, Jesus acknowledged the power of faith in two people, the woman and Jarius. Then, He performed two miracles, ignored those who ridiculed Him and conquered time.

He did it again much later, but on the second occasion, instead of postponing a visit by an hour or so, he postponed a visit four days. It was then that Jesus, who conquered both death and time, paid a visit to Lazarus.

Day seventeen
JESUS, THE RESOLUTE ONE

In Matthew 20, Jesus encounters two blind men. They call out to Him, and He heals them. There. It's a tidy little cameo, a roadside event that makes us feel good about our Savior. The event gets only a few verses, and we might consider it to pale in comparison to what is about to happen in Chapter 21, but the caution is this, when we take something out of context, it leaves room for pretext, and pretext is just a five-dollar word for *opinion*.

The context of the story starts back in Mathew 19 when He enters Jericho, and it continues in Matthew 21 with the account of *the triumphal entry*. When taken as a whole, we begin to see the most profound aspects of the Messiah.

The story on the Jericho road is not incidental. While it is not *the triumphal entry* – it is about *the triumphal exit*. Jesus is leaving Jericho where he has been for fifty-eight verses (we don't know how long that is, perhaps weeks). In Jericho He teaches and gathers large crowds as He heals His way through the city. When He leaves, a multitude follows Him, probably in a ticker-tape parade atmosphere. You would think that Jesus would let them have their moment, after all they were properly acknowledging the King of Kings, but Jesus was at work.

He was resolute. He was always about His Father's business, and while it was not known to anyone other than Himself, *the triumphal exit* from Jericho led directly to *the triumphal entry* into Jerusalem. He was a week away from the Cross, the awful / beautiful act of the Last Lamb. Given the urgency of the moment, we assume He would be concentrating on things loftier than two ragged blind men disrupting the victory parade. If it was up to the multitude, He wouldn't have given the men the time of day – but thankfully – it is not up to the multitude. It is up to the Servant who never stops serving – who never stops worshipping the Father and who would never stop until the fullness of the Cross was complete.

This is good news – because no matter what is happening around us, He stops for our story.

Day eighteen
JESUS, THE INVADER

In the months before D-DAY, the allies prepared some bizarre machines designed to clear the way for the landing crafts on the beaches of Normandy. There was a giant roller-comb that spun up the coils of barbed wire. A 'crab machine' that cleared land mines and massive picker-grinders removed the jagged steel hedgehogs from the shallow water. Anything that would impede the invasion was addressed, with the goal of smoothing the way for the invasion.

John said, *make straight the way of the LORD*. It was another D-DAY, the original D-DAY. Heaven was invading earth with an invasion force of one, and to prepare men, John went behind enemy lines and made-ready the landing beaches. The invasion could penetrate quicker, deeper and more profoundly if the hearts of men were cleared of rubble of doubt. When disbelief is swept aside, and when the obstacles of legalism are removed, the good news is free to advance.

Basically, John was saying that men of faith were wanted to assist in the invasion. Everything was about to change, and men were going to be accountable for what they had seen and heard. Moreover, men were supposed to be watching for the fulfilment of prophecy, but many of them did not want to take part in the invasion. They had grown comfortable with the status quo, because the status quo reflected nicely on themselves. They had been lulled into legalism, the belief that the behavior of man was key to salvation. In other words, man was his own savior, and God would recognize the attempts of obedience and reward him accordingly.

Still, there was a recollection of prophecy that promised the Messiah. From heaven would come the remedy, and to many leaders of the day, that meant the overthrow of the oppression of Rome. Overthrowing Rome would have been profound, but generally the thoughts of man pale in comparison to the thoughts of God. The Messiah did not come to overthrow Rome, He came to overthrow the real enemy and redeem mankind forever.

In Jesus' ministry, the Sadducees viewed him as a Pharisee, and the Pharisees viewed him as a dangerous radical. John the Baptist got it right. He viewed Jesus as *the Lamb of God who takes away the sin of the world.*

Day nineteen
JESUS, THE UNCOMPROMISED

Jesus is teaching in the Temple when the chief priests come to him and say, "Do you have permission to teach here?" Reading between the lines, we can hear them say, "This is *our* Temple. Who gave you authority?"

Jesus considered His answer. He could have played the trump card and said, "The Father sent me. Yahweh ordained my mission – and by the way – what do you mean *your temple*? This was built using stone that I created." He could have said that. In the flesh, you and I probably would have been indignant, but look carefully how Jesus answered. He knew who He was dealing with and He went to the core of the question by asking, "What do you really believe? Declare yourself - the baptism of John, was it of man or God?"

At this point, the priests demonstrated a tragic lack of nerve, which grew out of an exaggerated sense of self-protection. They withdrew and conferred with each other to try to find the most agreeable answer. Since protecting their position was more important than revelation, they said, "We do not know." In that moment they became spiritually vacuous by finding a compromise that was somewhere between charity and contempt.

If they had known that the ultimate security in the universe was standing in front of them, they would have considered no other answer, but Jesus saw that they were not ready. They had no desire to understand the greater truth, and Jesus' answer was perfect for the time and place. He would not aggravate a person who was (at the moment) incapable of changing his mind.

Revelation is given to a person when he is ready to welcome it. When it comes, the person is asked to change something to make room for it. This usually entails getting rid of something old and comfortable and replace it with something daring and just a little freaky. It is the way the Kingdom is advanced, one wonderfully peculiar, but often perplexing download at a time.

There is no end to His revelation. It is inexhaustible, and it is new every morning. It is like getting in an elevator of a building with no top floor.

Day twenty
THE BLOOD OF JESUS

For God was pleased to have all His fullness dwell in Him, and through Him to reconcile to Himself all things, whether on earth or things in heaven, by making peace through His blood, shed on the cross. Colossians 1:19

In the Garden of Eden, sin placed all of creation at odds with God and His plan. Adam and Eve ate of the tree of the knowledge of good and evil in spite of the warning that if they did, *they would surely die.* Suddenly they knew sin, and with it the awful realization that they were cut off from sinless God.

Sin swallows up life, and life is required to pay sin's debt. In Leviticus 17, it says, *the life of the flesh is in the blood, and I have given it unto you upon the altar to make atonement for your souls. It is the blood that makes atonement for the soul.* Blood is the life of man and animal - therefore sacrifice is a life for a life. Atonement is the proper act of a person taking steps to correct a wrongdoing. It begins with remorse, and it entails a desire to once again be at-one-with (atone) the One who was wronged. But our blood is contaminated with sin, which means there cannot be a total remission of sins. While shedding our blood would be worthy as an attempt at atonement, it is not sufficient. At the

Cross, Christ restored harmony and fellowship. When we receive Jesus, we receive the bond of peace the New Covenant.

The blood of Jesus was superior to the cumulative shedding of blood under the Old Covenant. Jesus blood satisfied the requirements of the Father. His blood is forever, the agency for forgiveness, cleansing, healing, redemption and deliverance.

Shame on me for thinking it was not for me – and double the shame for taking it lightly. St. Augustine said, *Don't hold yourselves cheap, seeing that the Creator of all things (and of me) estimates my value so high and so dear that He pours out the precious blood of His only begotten Son.*

There's power, power, wonder working power in the precious blood of the Lamb.

Day twenty-one
JESUS, THE PROPITIATION, part one

When you love something extravagantly, you hate the thing that keeps you apart from it. You will do anything to eliminate the separator. In a garden a long time ago, a man and a woman used the free-will that God gave them, to do something God hates. They sinned, and God hates sin because it separates the sinner from Him.

Zapping sin (and Satan) out of existence would seem logical to you and me, but God always conforms to His own attributes, and justice – even to the enemy – is an integral of His nature. In other words, it is not in His nature to annihilate sin simply because it would be convenient. Instead, He acts according to His perfect character, whether in joy or in grief.

Right and wrong matter. When we know 'right' and do 'wrong', there's a consequence; and prior to the Cross of Jesus, for thousands of years, people of almost every religious notion felt the need to make amends for their shortcomings. The ancient Hebrew did it by animal sacrifices to Yahweh. The Canaanites sacrificed to Molech, the Philistines to Dagon and the Egyptians sacrificed to any number of gods. Original sin led to original shame, and over the millennia, a river of blood was spilled trying to make things (momentarily) right between God and man.

Some ancient cultures had this 'right' knowledge but applied it in the most horrific way. Their answer was to sacrifice something more valuable than an animal, and the awful practice of human sacrifice was the outcome. Strangely enough, they had the right concept. The sacrifice that really matters is the one that is the most personal and valuable. This kind of thinking invites men to compete for the size and nature of the sacrifice, and it is at this point that we discover the operative truth; *whoever has the most to lose, is in a position to pay the highest price.*

In the personage of Jesus, the question of the 'highest sacrifice' is answered forever. It is the end of the competition. No person in history could sacrifice what God can sacrifice. If Jesus had not (willingly) paid the price, God could not claim to be a God of love. Instead, He would be a hesitant, self-protecting god who regrets creating His creation in the first place.

Day twenty-two
JESUS, THE PROPITIATION, part 2

Jesus gave up his deity to be born in the flesh. This was His first sacrifice. Throughout His ministry, He gave up His supernatural powers by emptying Himself of His divine nature. Then He gave up His life by enduring an extraordinarily cruel execution. Still, that was not the truly majestic sacrifice. Men do this. Not often, but once in a while a good man will lay down his life for another. Jesus did this for all men, but the agonizing death on the Cross was not the utmost sacrifice.

Another, even greater sacrifice was made. Jesus gave up purity. The creator of the universe – the author of love, truth, goodness and righteousness, invited sin into death with Himself. Just as iron filings are attracted to a magnet, sin was drawn to the Darling of Heaven. Jesus became sin, and when He died, the power of sin died with Him, defeated forever.

For the Father, the sacrifice of His Son was so perfect – so eternally sufficient that God's wrath against sin was extinguished. Jesus wore our sin, then he transported it to the bowels of hell where it belongs. As majestic as that is, it still does not represent Jesus' most glorious sacrifice.

Just before He died, Jesus suffered His greatest loss. He lost relationship with the Father. God, who cannot be partner to sin, separated Himself from relationship with the Son. At this moment, Jesus utters the only lament of the Cross, *My God, My God, why have you forsaken me?* The separation from the Father was so great, so unspeakably profound, that it broke Jesus' heart.

God's wrath was aimed at the thing that separated Him from the creatures He loved - and finally, His wrath was satisfied. It is called 'propitiation', the act of becoming well-disposed toward a thing. The wall was torn down between God and man. For the first time since Eden, intimate relationship with God was available to all of humankind.

Sin held dual powers. It was the thing that kept man away from righteousness, and it was the thing that kept God from enjoying intimacy with His creation. If you believe this – that is, if you believe the Cross of Jesus was the act that defeated the power of sin, and you confess it – then you are saved.

Day twenty-three
THE VINYARD AND THE CROSS

A good way to understand a parable is to make it personal. Put yourself in the story and see what emotions make it to the surface. In Matthew 20 is the story of the landowner who spent much of a day hiring laborers. The lucky guys who were hired at three in the afternoon were paid as much as the guys who started sweating at nine in the morning. If the landowner had paid the workers privately, there would have been no problem, but he didn't. The nine a.m. workers were indignant, even though they had agreed to the wages. They agreed to something - and were fine with it until they saw somebody else getting special treatment. Indignation took the place of agreement.

Did the landlord act unfairly? Did he show favoritism? And if he did, what business is it of ours? The parable was the teaching, but in a short time, Jesus would take the same spiritual truth and make it a demonstration. For the scribes, Pharisees and other mockers of Jesus, what He said on the cross must have been an insult. The leaders of the synagogue, the supposed spiritual leaders of the Jews, spent their lives practicing law abidance and sin management. They were obese with pride over their own righteous accomplishments, and suddenly on the Cross, the one who proclaimed to be the Messiah, said to a thief hanging next to him, "Today, you will be with me in paradise."

"The nerve of this pretender!" The scorners might have said. "How dare him suggest that a thief, who probably served no synagogue time, perhaps knew little scripture, and for sure was a breaker of the law - - how could such a man share paradise with the righteous elite? If they had heard Jesus' parable, they would have heard that the worker who put in one hour, was afforded the same pay as the man who labored all day.

What do we do with it? Do we say UNFAIR! Do we say, "I've been teaching Sunday School for twenty years, and I deserve preferential treatment?" Or do we celebrate the Savior Redeemer who saves and redeems no matter how full our time-card is?"

Day twenty-four
I WANT SOME OF THAT!

Jesus is in the region of Tyre and Sidon. He had been in the land of Gennesaret (Southern Galilee) but between verses He walked some forty miles to visit the Gentiles. If I was a disciple, I would expect great things to come of a trip like that, maybe another feeding of thousands of people, or perhaps some walking on water, but what they got for their eighty-mile round trip, was a Gentile woman who was a nuisance.

She was a pest, apparently so annoying that the disciples tried to get Jesus to send her away. Jesus said to them (not to her) that He was *not sent except to the lost sheep of Israel,* which was a curious thing to say since they were in Gentile territory. It isn't recorded in the narrative, but we can imagine the disciples grumbling, *then why are we even here*? The reason they were there, was Kingdom business. With the Son of Man, everything was Kingdom business, and something was happening between the flesh and the Father that only Jesus could discern.

When the annoying woman worshipped him, she demonstrated her heart. What Jesus told the woman is music – perhaps the most beautiful thing any seeker can hear from the lips of the Messiah. "Great is your faith." He said, "let it be to you as you desire."

As always, there is more to a story that sits on the surface. It could be that Jesus went up to the region because at one time, centuries earlier, the entire region of Phoenicia (Tyre and Sidon) was a part of the allocation of the land given to the tribe of Asher. Asher was supposed to take the land and make it prosper. They failed, and the woman (the pest) became a lost sheep of the house of Israel.

Moreover, Jesus was demonstrating, if not to the multitudes, then to the disciples. They made an eighty-mile round trip for one lost sheep, and just to make sure the lesson was learned, Jesus did it again when he crossed the Sea of Galilee to the Decapolis. There, he ministered to one exceedingly annoying, crazy person – the howler of the tombs.

Day twenty-five
JESUS, THE SON OF DAVID

The Bible has its nerve. If it was left to the whims of the flesh, we would have long ago edited out huge swaths of scripture. Gone would be any mention of biblical heroes with feet of clay. Gone would be the record of supposedly godly people, acting badly. After all, the shortcomings of our heroes serve as ammunition for the skeptics, and you would think that over the centuries, we would edit out the narratives that were indelicate. Think how clean it would be. On the cutting room floor would be the story of Samson, part of the story of Judah, Abraham, Moses, Jacob and Saul. David himself would have to be edited, and eventually we would end up with the antiseptic accounts of Elijah, Ruth, Esther, Caleb, Daniel and other role model exemplars.

Thankfully, the Author (the Holy Spirit) protected Holy Scripture from the editors. It is not our job or anybody's job to make the Bible nicer. It is a picture of us, and our desperate need for a Savior / Redeemer, and face it – in the flesh we are not entirely nice. Scripture has its nerve. It risks real life stories that horrify the reader, and it features stories of radicals and zealots going against the popular culture of the day. We might be embarrassed by them, but the story is told for our benefit, and shame on us for trying to renovate it to soothe our sensitivities.

David is the poster boy for a hero who with smudges. In spite of his defects, he is revered, and we have powerful Old Testament prophecies that the Messiah would be regarded as the Son of David. Why? Because David is a picture of the kind of kingship Jesus has in mind for you and me.

Jesus *is* the Son of David, both genealogically and figuratively. The very best parts of David are a foretaste of Jesus.

- He is the warrior king, the conqueror.
- He is the leader of men who willingly followed him, no matter where it took them.
- He was a king who preferred the ephod of the priest, instead of the robe of the monarch.
- He was the king who established worship as his first act of kingship.
- He was the king who ached over his lost children.
- And he was the king who wept, and then towered over his enemy.

Day twenty-six
JESUS, AND THE 2nd BEST MAN

Earlier we speculated on the existence of the second best, and now is a good time to consider his predicament. Somewhere, at some time in history this man lived, and we can imagine him presenting his case to God. He might argue that on the whole, he was the second best whoever drew breath and with that resume, he should be allowed entry into heaven.

What would the Father do? Would He invite this pretty good man into His heaven? Sorry, but no. God's realm is perfect, and no matter how a man might try to cover his sin with good deeds and righteous behavior, underneath it all - is sin. Adam was pretty good in the garden. He only sinned once, but that one sin got him banished. We might not like it, in fact, many people are offended by it, and in their insult, they cry UNFAIR. They argue that God gave man free-will and when man didn't use it in a way that pleased Him – he was banished! What's up with that?

The reality is this - right and wrong matter, and there is a reward for doing right and a penalty for doing wrong. We know this. It is in us, and in an effort to make up for our defects, we tried everything to pay the price. We were imprisoned by sin, but we were ultimately helpless to come up with the bail. Still, as we know, bail is one thing, and the trial is another. Bail does not exonerate us, it only defers judgment. If only we could make the sin disappear, now that would be something.

Consider a metaphor: Pour a glass of uncontaminated milk, then add a dash of pepper. A dash will do because after all, it's a good class of milk. You might be able to convince people that it's alright, but you know different. The pepper is in there, it is sin, and it cannot be removed by any effort of man. Somehow, the milk has to be changed. It cannot be refined or filtered or otherwise treated. You cannot counsel the milk to become pure and you cannot simply add more milk to dilute the impurity. It has to be changed, just as we have to be changed. We must become a new creation…one in which old things are passed away and all things become new.

We are cleansed by the blood, and while we still sin, we confess it, and herein lies the majesty. When we confess, it is the sin that is banished, not the man.

Day twenty-seven
WHAT'S THE PRICE?

He is the father of lies, the originator of sin, the enemy of God and the holder of dominion from Eden to Calvary. He is the spellbinder who bewitched man into sin. He convinced Adam and Eve that God was holding out on them – that God knew things they did not know – and if they ate from the forbidden tree, they would be like God. It was the paleo lie.

In the garden, Adam and Eve agreed with the liar. Previously, they had been given dominion over earth, and dominion means they had it in their possession, and could freely give it away if they chose. They chose poorly, and Satan took dominion from them. Mind you, God was still sovereign, but the enemy had dominion up until the time it could be repossessed. Adam and Eve and every human descendant had been kidnapped and found themselves desperately in need of a rescuer.

Who was paying the price?	God
What was the price?	Jesus
Who was Jesus paying?	The Father
Who was it for?	You and me
Why pay it to the Father?	To extinguish His wrath against sin
Why?	To repair the separation

In the singular act of the Cross, God lifted the death sentence. The wages of sin was (is) no longer death, instead it is life, and life abundant. The Cross of Jesus is the centerpiece of the history of humankind. It forever changed the condition of mortal man.

- Dominion was repossessed. It was handed back to man and the original command to 'subdue the earth' was back in effect.
- With dominion back where it belonged, the Holy Spirit was free to occupy anyone who sought Him.
- Man was free to live under grace.
- The enemy discovered the price the Father was willing to pay. It was not good news for Satan, but unbelievably good news for humankind.
- Man's double loss was restored. We now have relationship with God and rulership under God. Love wins.

Day twenty-eight
JESUS, THE EQUALIZER

Some insist on holding onto the first century Hebrew view on women and their 'proper' place in society and in the church. Paul talked about it, but Jesus said nothing. While He didn't speak on the topic, He did something more profound, He demonstrated. He was fulfilling the law, making possible the shift from legalism to love.

Jesus was always demonstrating, and we are well served to pay attention to His demonstrations. Typical of this is His implied regard for women. On five occasions, He held a one-on-one conference with a woman. Five different women came to Jesus and were alone with Him, away from the disciples or any other person. In these private encounters, Jesus imparted special revelation. Five powerful, transcendent truths were entrusted to women who otherwise might not have had the chance to see Him because they were stuck in the nursery or confined to the kitchen.

We have no business confining anybody to a lesser station simply because of gender, race or heritage. This doesn't say that authority and leadership are granted to everyone, but it does say that everyone has an equal shot at it.

America, the land of the free, is also the home of five national smudges. All of them have roots in the notion of inequality. We claim to be working on them, but some of them have been part of our culture for so long that we have developed a distorted generational worldview. The smudges are: 1) the way we treated the indigenous peoples, 2) slavery, 3) the way we treated immigrants, the Chinese and Irish in particular, 4) the way we treated women, and 5) the way we treat the unborn.

....

If we applied the words and demonstrations of Jesus, to how it is that we consider each other – what would America look like? *If My people who are called by My name will humble themselves, and pray and seek My face, and turn from their wicked ways, then I will hear from heaven, and will forgive their sin and heal their land. 2 Chronicles, 7-14*

Day twenty-nine
JESUS, THE RE-CREATOR

There's a TV program called 'the Repair Shop'. People bring treasures that are broken or missing parts or are just worn out, and the artisans and craftsmen go to work. Their goal is to make the heirloom as good as new, or almost, and they do incredible work. When they're done, the vase or toy train or gramophone looks brand new, but of course they know it isn't. Somewhere in the vase is a patched crack, a glued-on handle or touch-up ceramic paint.

It's us. Adam started it. When he sinned, he was no longer new, and he knew it. When he broke the commandment, he broke himself, and in the temporal world, the adage is this, you break it – you fix it. Adam's descendants, for thousands of years, tried to fix it. While offering sacrifices and keeping the law pieced man back together, he was still broken. The cracks showed and there was nothing he could do to make himself new again…

…until Jesus. He didn't patch us back together – He made a way for us to become a new creation. *Old things have passed away, and behold all things became new.*

Creating is an integral part of God's nature. We were made in His image, which means we are the product of the dust of the earth and the breath of God. Our created imprint means we were meant to engage in both realms, the spiritual and the temporal. Some say that creation is on-going, and we are proof of it.

Believing in the Lord Jesus Christ changes a man, and it is very clear that at the Cross, we were not changed into a new creature, we became a restored creation, once more holy and acceptable in His sight. God looks upon us and does not see the patched crack, or the glue that shows up on the x-ray. He finds no flaws in us because we have taken on the flawless one, and in Him we enjoy all the benefits that come with redemption.

Sure, we sin, but it is the residue of the fallen soul – the habits of the flesh and the echoes of old addictions and dependencies. Working these out of our behavior is the process of working out our salvation. Please, don't misunderstand this. We do not work out *the act of being saved*. We are saved! What we work out is the fullness of it, and this just might be what occupies us throughout eternity. It is for certain, more than we can think or imagine – and that should excite us, forever.

Day thirty
JESUS, THE ROCK

People of any age and any skill level can climb a rock…indoors. The climber is safely harnessed, protected from danger and is provided hand and toe grips all the way. Advanced climbers don't need the harnesses, and elite climbers don't need the hand and toe grips. These extravagant climbers can scale El Capitan by finding the tiniest and most tenuous grips. But what about a rock face that is a sheer ninety degrees – a perfectly smooth face with no cracks, crevices, ledges, or any irregularity at all. Forget it! It can't be scaled.

Like it or not, you and I have crevices, creases and ledges. They are irregularities, gripping points that provide a strong hold. We are not perfect, and the enemy works tirelessly to conquer us. He wants to proclaim victory over us, and very often we allow it. We provide the hand and toe holds and sometimes we even throw him a rope.

Jesus left His cousin John at the Jordan. He was filled with the Spirit and the Spirit led Him to the wilderness where the tempter came and tried to find a foothold. He (the devil) tried everything common to man, but the temptations that worked perfectly for thousands of years did not work on Jesus. Even the ultimate temptation failed. "I will give you everything if you worship me," Satan said. It was not an empty promise. Satan had dominion over everything on earth. It was in fact, his to give away - - and Jesus rebuked him saying, "You shall not tempt the LORD your God." Dominion is one thing, and Sovereignty is quite another.

The enemy failed. Jesus was a sheer ninety-degree rock wall with no gripping points. He had no crevices or flaws into which a stronghold could wedge itself. Later, in a remarkable statement about Himself, Jesus said to the devil, "You have nothing on Me," and the devil knew it was true.

In the telling of the temptation (Matthew and Luke), it is evident that the devil was nervous. He knew full well who he was dealing with. It was the Son of Man, God incarnate, the Sovereign One who had come to repossess the lost domain. Satan was close to panic. He had been put on notice.

Day thirty-one
IRRESISTIBLE, part one

In the fall of 2016, a frenzy spread across North America. It was the sudden revival of what was once a most agreeable thing - but had faded from favor. Little by little the common notion was, that this thing had become old fashioned. It had outlived its usefulness, and it no longer met the needs of a sophisticated generation.

But if a thing is inherently good, it will endure, and in early November 2016, a remarkable event occurred. An unexpected moment grabbed the attention of the country. Those few people who still loved the old thing suddenly found themselves in the company of people who were asking for it to be explained.

It was a revival. Something unusual was happening that was beyond the ability of many people to understand. It was so compelling, that skeptics were caught up in it. It was baseball. The Chicago Cubs, after a draught of 108 years, were about to win the World Series. While we shouldn't trivialize spiritual revival with something as temporal as baseball, the analogy is too good to pass up, besides, Thomas Boswell was right when he said, *'Life imitates the World Series."*

On the night of game seven of the World Series, more people watched the game, as watched everything else – combined on television. This massive audience certainly included millions of people who were not fans but would consider becoming one. They were fascinated, and full of questions, and it is possible that they turned to baseball fans for answers. They asked things they thought they would never ask because suddenly, what they were watching was captivating, and it was somehow personal.

Clearly, it was infectious, and that in a word, is revival. People aren't coerced into it or shamed into it, instead they are captured by it. It is Jesus who is irresistible, and it is His church, properly positioned and equipped that is given the joy of discipling newcomers and shepherding a new community of believers.

Day thirty-two
IRRESISTIBLE, part two

People by the thousands collected to see Jesus, and why not. He healed, and at that time in ancient Judea, there was no shortage of patients. It's my guess that not everybody who came to see Jesus was interested in His theology, which is why the pattern for His ministry was to demonstrate Himself before He explained Himself. He healed the people! It didn't seem to matter how long it took, and when He was done, He looked out over a crowd that was primed and anxious to receive a Kingdom message.

I wonder what the impact of His homily would have been had He not properly introduced Himself. His audience consisted of people who gave up a day and walked miles just to be there. Some came to satisfy a curiosity, some for healing and some to confirm a suspicion. We know that some were sent to investigate, and even to scorn. But no matter the motive of the audience, the message never changed.

The man whose leprosy spots disappear will probably listen to the man who made them disappear, and before you think that it was different because it was 'Jesus' that did it by Himself, think again. Christendom nearly atrophied under the idea that - while we have hope, we are lacking in power and authority. For centuries, we leaned on a wobbly theology, a mentality that weakens the church and in time makes it no more spiritually productive than a fraternity. Thankfully, that's not how Jesus saw it. He consistently deferred to the Father and the Spirit, and that's why He was able to look into His disciple's eyes and say, *"What you see me doing, you also will do."*

Peter, the one who was with Jesus for three and a half years and was willing to die for Him, was taken down by a servant girl. When push came to shove, Peter denied Jesus. Why? It is because for years he had Jesus, but he didn't yet have what Jesus had. Fifty days after his denial, Peter got it. Jesus operated in the Spirit, and at Pentecost, so did Peter. Suddenly, the words, *what see me doing, you also will do,"* made sense. From that moment on, Peter, like his Master Jesus, was irresistible.

In this day and age, as in every day and age, Jesus is telling you and me, *you have what I had, now go and do what I did.*

Day thirty-three
JESUS, SON OF MAN, Part one

Jesus was in every way man – and in every way God – except for one magnificent difference. In an inconceivably sublime act, He willingly forfeited his divine nature, and chose instead to operate on earth exclusively as man. He was sinless but was otherwise subject to the temptations of man. In this scenario, there was no violation of the rules of engagement with the enemy. The fight was not between God and Satan - they've already had that fight and Satan lost. No, this fight was between man and the accuser.

Everything Jesus did, He did as man. It could not be otherwise. He was not Clark Kent, changing into tights and a cape when superpowers were needed. Jesus did toggle between man and God. If Jesus conducted himself in His divine nature, why would He have to pray? Why would He have to be baptized?

Yes, He was God, but so long as He was in earthly skin, He was man. Time after time, Jesus diminished Himself saying, *it is not me...but the Father who is in me.* On at least two occasions, He was tempted. He was subject to hunger and thirst. He slept and played and stubbed His toes, and He experienced pain. Think about it - if He shifted between human and divine natures, He could have experienced the Cross without enduring the pain of it. Where is the sacrifice in that? This, incidentally, was the final verbal taunt (temptation) from the accuser. The thief on the cross next to him scorned Him, saying, *if you are really who you say you are, come down from there.* The thief had no idea of the magnitude of the event – the reality that as Jesus hung there, it was exactly where He purposed to be in the flesh.

We don't have it in us to conjure a story of this majesty, or even to think the thought, because we cannot conceive of the nature of the uncontaminated One. It is not in us to conceive perfect love, the love with no boundaries. It is simply too big a thought – and strangely, that is good news. I do not want to serve a Savior Redeemer who is small enough for me to comprehend.

Day thirty-four
JESUS, THE SON OF MAN, part two

The story is in the Bible. It actually happened, but what is not in the narrative, is a peek at the dynamic behind the scenes. Jesus was walking with His guys in Galilee, and it serves us well to properly picture this slice of reality. Jesus was probably not wearing a clean white robe, with a smart-looking blue tunic. He didn't own a Hebrew smoking jacket and there was not a halo hovering over His head everywhere He went. He had purpose, but he probably did not stride purposefully, hands folded with his little troop following reverently (and quietly) behind.

No. They're guys, all of them, except one of them is the Son of Man. They're friends. They've been together for three years, and last night Bartholomew had trouble starting the fire and he's getting some ribbing. Peter, who lost a wrestling match to Thomas, was looking for another chance at the guy. Jesus was the referee for the match, and for the moment, He is just one of the thirteen – but He is the one who is plugged-in, tuned-in and perfectly in sync with the Holy Spirit. Jesus' spirit was fully mature, and it (His spirit) was the receiver of wisdom, counsel, knowledge and power. The conduit was wide open, constantly. In Himself, Jesus was in the natural realm, but in the Spirit, He interacted in the supernatural. The power Jesus demonstrated was not His own – but was from God flowing through Him. His spirit was the place where physics was interwoven with metaphysics.

On their walk in Galilee, the Holy Spirit speaks to Jesus. "Two lepers, five-hundred yards ahead," the Spirit says. Jesus nods. He knows what to do with a download like that. The Holy Spirit is about to show off, and God is going to demonstrate Himself through the Son of Man.

In this narrative, Jesus did the opposite of what the culture required. He not only approached the lepers, but He broke the law by touching them. Then, knowing that the Holy Spirit had in mind something from the Kingdom, Jesus spoke healing on the men. Jesus, who emptied Himself of his divine nature, relied entirely on the Holy Spirit, since supernatural healing required supernatural attention. This is the reason Jesus was able to explain to his troop that "What you see me doing – you also will do." Little did the disciples know that someday soon, they would have what Jesus had, the indwelling of the Holy Spirit. You want some good news today? This is Good News.

Day thirty-five
JESUS, THE SON OF MAN, part 3

Jesus was the only one who could rightfully represent both kingdoms. As the Son of Man, He was the last and perfect Lamb, and as Creator He was the Anointed One, empowered to prepare the way for the Kingdom. Everything Adam possessed, except a sinless nature, was returned to man, and today when we say 'yes' to Jesus, we are saying 'yes' to restoration. We become new, a reconciled creation with a regenerated heart. God's wrath against sin was extinguished at the Cross and we are, once again acceptable.

- **John 1:14:** The Word became flesh and made his dwelling among us. We have seen his glory, the glory of the one and only Son, who came from the Father, full of grace and truth.
- **John 5: 19, 20:** Jesus gave them this answer: I tell you the truth, the Son can do nothing by himself; he can do only what he sees his Father doing, because whatever the Father does the Son also does.
- **John 5:30:** By myself I can do nothing; I judge only as I hear, and my judgment is just, for I seek not to please myself but him who sent me.
- **John 7:16:** Jesus answered, "My teaching is not my own. It comes from Him who sent me."

- **John 12:** For I did not speak of my own accord, but the Father who sent me commanded me what to say and how to say it.
- **John 14:10 & 11:** The words I say to you are not just my own. Rather, it is the Father, living in me, who is doing his work. Believe me when I say that I am in the Father and the Father is in me; or at least believe on the evidence of the miracles themselves.
- **John 14:12:** I tell you the truth, anyone who has faith in me will do what I have been doing. He will do even greater things than these, because I am going to the Father.
- **Phil. 2: 6,7:** (Jesus) Who, being in very nature God, did not consider equality with God something to be used to his own advantage; rather, he made himself nothing by taking the very nature of a servant, being made in human likeness.

And many, many more verses and validations.

Day thirty-six
JESUS, THE SON OF MAN, Part 4

Christianity is the only religion that has as its central event, the public humiliation of God. At the Cross, in the face of scorn and disgrace, Jesus took on sin. He wore it. He absorbed it all so that He could carry it to the grave and dispose of it. Jesus became the thing that God hates…sin. And when it was done, when this exquisite price had been paid by the flawless Lamb, one drop of the blood of Jesus became more powerful than the accumulated filth of all of humankind for all time. It is not possible that God would allow any sin to be greater than His Son's payment for it. If God's wrath against sin was greater than His love for His creation, the Cross would have no meaning because love would have been compromised. The Cross was the act that also satisfied the requirements of justice. At long last, at the resurrection, God not only had just-cause to come against the enemy, He had the legal right to do so. Here is the summary.

- In the first Garden, God gave Adam and Eve dominion over earth. Satan was an interloper.
- Adam and Eve were supposed to subdue the earth and demonstrate their dominion.
- The enemy convinced them to follow his advice, not that of God.

- Once given dominion, man was free to give it away. The act of sin handed dominion over to the enemy where it was held for thousands of years. Remember, while Satan had dominion. God was still Sovereign.
- The price of it (the wages of sin) is death. Death could not be defeated until sin was defeated – and sin could not be defeated until a suitable price was paid. Man was incapable of paying such a price. We tried, but always came up short.
- At the resurrection, sin was deposited in hell. Sin was defeated and God's wrath against sin was forever extinguished.
- The thing that separated God from His beloved creation (you and me) was removed, and dominion was handed back to its rightful owner, mankind.
- God is love. He is serious about us. We are the centerpiece of His creation and now we are invited to get what He intended for us, both here (dominion and power) and in the here-after (citizenship in heaven).

Day thirty-seven
JESUS, THE PILOT FOR THE KINGDOM

In 1966, it was announced that the Starship Enterprise would go where no man had gone before. Hmmm. Some two thousand years earlier, Jesus said *"Go with me and I'll take you to places where no man has gone before."* Granted, the two promises sound the same, but there's a big difference. The 1966 proclamation was fictional, but the original promise was real. The real one is the other Kingdom, the superior reality. It is governed by a truth that is exempt from decay, compromise, misinterpretation, contamination and death. When our universe comes to an end (and science and the Bible assures us that it will someday), truth will be the residue. If you are tempted to say, *so what - there will not be anybody around to observe it* - have a different thought!

The Kingdom of God is not some smallish reality that has boundaries. It is not constricted to fit into a small space that is only 14 billion light years across. It is independent of space and time. The Kingdom of God is not a reality that depends on anything physical or temporal. It does not rely on the four fundamental forces and other physical laws of nature. The existence of the Kingdom is not dependent on a sun to produce warmth, or plants to produce oxygen. Like it or not, all physical conditions are *time dependent*, which makes everything in the universe transitory and temporary. God, who made it all and is in it all, is also outside of it all. To our reckoning, the universe is incomprehensibly huge, but to God, it must seem smallish. The universe, which we think of as massive and breathtaking, is His trinket, and this little physical realm is a demonstration of His majesty. We live in it, but most men only live in only a small understanding of it.

To expand our experience, there's a border we are invited to cross. It is where this reality ends and a superior reality begins - and no - a person doesn't have to be dead to go there. Imagine a place where there is no such thing as fear, a place where we trust our leader implicitly, because our leader is perfect in every way.

Believe in Him, and like the captain of your plane, He says, *good morning - we have gained altitude, and you are now free to move about the Kingdom.*

Day thirty-eight
THE KINGDOM

The Kingdom of God cannot display itself without upsetting the temporal world. The Kingdom is a troublemaker, because at its core, it is disruptive. It proposes a different comfort, a different security and a different allegiance. It exhibits a worldview that is sure to irritate a humanistic culture. It does not do this on purpose, but there it is – it cannot and will not change. It is already perfect. It is the superior reality working to get the attention of a defiled world.

The Kingdom will not compromise its message just to appease a fickle society. In our culture, we compromise because we think we have to, and the end result is usually predictable. We find that we have settled for a middle ground that is mutually unsatisfactory to both parties. Not so with matters that apply to the Kingdom. It is not possible to domesticate God, however we live in a culture that seems to want to do that. It is vacuous to dilute God down to something 'nice', something gentle and kindly. It is an insult to the Kingdom, and it when the church does it, it is indicative of a tragic loss of nerve.

The Kingdom is sublimely contrary. It is where the last will be first, where the meek will inherit the earth. It is where light overpowers darkness and where the highest station is in being a servant. Finally, it is where the hero of all humankind marches into pitched battle with the villain of all humankind, and the hero insists on dying.

The Kingdom is at hand. The enemy has nothing on Jesus, and this should be our objective, to live so in step with the Kingdom that we can say to the enemy, *you have nothing on me.* In the last days, Jesus will overthrow the enemy, but He will not do it alone. The Church, properly engaging the power and authority He gave it, will once again *make straight the way for the Lord.*

Reducing it down to basics; in Psalm 103, God tells us to forget not His benefits. There are five things God is prepared to do for us - forgive our sins, heal our diseases, redeem our souls from the pit, crown us with loving kindness and satisfy us with good things. Turn to the Gospels, and Jesus says there are five things we are encouraged to do for Him - preach the Kingdom, confess our sins, heal the sick, destroy the works of the enemy and love our neighbor.

Day thirty-nine
AMAZING MERCY,
HOW SWEET THE SOUND

We sing Amazing Grace, and we should also sing Amazing Mercy. As near as we can tell, the first attribute that God put on display, was mercy. Even before His initial demonstration of love, God modeled mercy. Lucifer and his army lost the Paradise War, and they were exiled – not extinguished. In spite of the fact that this put the enemy in our back yard, it is an astonishing demonstration. God is just, and merciful even to his enemy, and strangely, that is good news. Later, God does it again. He declares that the wages of sin is death, and yet upon sinning, Adam and Eve did not die. In exile from the garden, Adam was given nearly a millennium to consider his choice.

Finally, at the Cross, Jesus (again) defeated Satan. Satan, now a two-time loser and soon to be a three-time loser, lost dominion over earth. Jesus took back the keys of earth. While He always held sovereignty, He was once again the Sovereign who ruled on a legitimate throne. And yet, the enemy is still at work! If Satan has been defeated – if death has lost its grip – why does the enemy still have power? Here is the good part, the part where we praise Jesus with all that is within us. Yes, Jesus is victorious, and yes, He calls all men to Him, and in doing this He invites us to share in the victory. We are to renounce the loser, declare partnership with the Victor and mop up the battlefield.

At the resurrection, Jesus could have easily extinguished the enemy. Dominion was wrestled away from Satan and was again properly invested to man. The fact that the enemy survived is the paradox of perfect mercy. Humankind was damaged by the enemy, and now with power, authority and dominion handed back to us, it is our turn to do damage to the enemy. Jesus explicitly told us to destroy the works of the enemy. Note, we do not get to extinguish Satan, Jesus gets to do that, but until he does, we, the Church, have the extraordinary assignment of disarming the hordes of evil.

Paul says to be more than conquerors. The only way to do more than defeat the enemy in battle, is to be such a constant threat that the enemy doesn't bother to show up. Now, that's cool!

Day forty
JESUS, THE FINISHER

There is one recorded lament at the Cross. At the end, Jesus cried out to the Father, "Why have you forsaken me?" It was (presumably) the moment when Jesus came into full identification with sinners (you and me). As He wore the sin of the world, the Father, who can have nothing to do with sin, separated from the Son. It was not that it was too awful to watch, or that His great heart was about to break, instead the separation was necessary for God's wrath against sin to be satisfied. We cannot conceive the anguish of the Father at the moment that He suspended communion and relationship with the Son. If ever there was a moment when love triumphed over anguish, this was it, and the wonder is that God did it for us. *For God so loved the world…that he gave his only begotten Son.*

With the price paid, God no longer held sin in contempt. We become – in his eyes, justified – whiter than snow and once again suitable for a relationship with God and rulership under God.

With the final words, "It is finished," everything on earth changed. From that spectacular moment on, there was a new sheriff in town. Satan had to forfeit authority over earth, and God's sovereignty over earth took on a new perspective that allowed the full release of the Holy Spirit. With dominion wrestled away from the enemy, the Spirit enjoyed the status of 'inhabitation' instead of 'visitation'. No longer did men have to sacrifice or do penance for sin. Redemption was achieved by trusting Jesus as Savior. *Believe in the Lord Jesus Christ, and you will be saved."*

Christianity is the only religion in which the supernatural paves the way through sacrifice. Soon after His lament, *my God, my God, why have you forsaken me*, Jesus uttered the superb words, *it is finished*. The words are breathtaking, and it is fitting that with the utterance, it actually took his breath. Jesus completed everything to the full satisfaction of the Father. He satisfactorily finished His work.

Hallelujah. The Cross is, and will always be, sufficient.

Day forty-one
JESUS OUR SAVIOR / REDEEMER

Many people don't know it yet, but there comes a time in almost every life when a man is desperate to be saved. For many men, the desperation is to be saved from death, but we know the truth on that one. It is appointed unto man once to die, and there is no escaping it. The Onion Newspaper recently ran a headline that read, *World Death Rate Holds Steady at 100 %.* It's true, and yet it still surprises people when it approaches.

Jesus does not save us from the death of the body. That was not the work of the Cross. Instead, He saves us into something vastly superior to our life as we know it – and then He saves us again into the stunning life that follows this one. A good question to ask a man is this, *are you fearful of death, or fearful of dying?* For me, if I have any apprehension at all, it would be a fear of dying. I want to be able to do it with nobility and grace. So far as a fear of death – Jesus took that one away. It has no sting, and the grave has no victory.

The Greek word for saved (salvation) is *sozo*. It is a powerful word, especially in the Greek, but over the centuries we have reduced it to mean forgiveness, and little else. Certainly, it is forgiveness, and that should never be diminished, but salvation (sozo) is much more. The broader definition of the word (sozo) encompasses forgiveness, healing and deliverance, all three. The three attributes share co-supremacy, and they are the glorious gift that pours from the Cross.

Forgiveness: *Believe in the Lord Jesus Christ and you will be saved (sozo).*
Healing: *Jesus turning and seeing her said 'Daughter take courage your faith has made you well (sozo) and at once the woman was made well (sozo).*
Deliverance: *And those who had seen it reported to them how the man who was demon-possessed had been made well (sozo).*

It's all ours. We are saved, healed and delivered all because of the preeminent Cross.

Day forty-two
JESUS, OUR BEST THOUGHT

There are two wolves in us. One of them is angry, short-tempered, easily offended and self-absorbed. The other wolf is kind, loving, sensitive and sacrificial. The wolves fight for control, and it is no secret which wolf wins.

> It is the one you feed.

Years ago, while on staff at a church in a small town, I was often asked to counsel some men. They shouldn't have asked. I am not gifted as a counselor, mostly because I am way too blunt – and yet, I think I did some good. My specialty seemed to be men with addictions, which was a topic to which I could personally relate. The typical session went like this:

He opens by saying, "I got this drinking problem, and I really want to quit."

I consider it for a moment, then about as subtle as a train wreck, I say, "No you don't. If you really wanted to quit, you'd quit."

He stiffens up, probably thinking I wasn't acting like a Christian should act. "Huh?' he says.

I'm on a roll. "We usually get what we want," I say, "when we want it bad enough, we get it."

He recollects himself and forms a defense. "But why doesn't God take it from me? I want Him to take it."

"You don't really mean that," I say, showing off my best counseling skills. "Think about it, do you really want a God who decides what you want and don't want?

"Yea."

"Well, He's not like that. He doesn't want to run your life – He wants you to – but He wants you to do the right thing."

"Then why doesn't he tell me the right thing?"

I don't hesitate, "Oh, he does," I say, "He stands at your door and knocks. Did you really think he'd come to your door and bust it down?"

"No," he said, self-consciously.

"You have to open the door. That's the deal. And when you do, Jesus has his hand out to take your addiction."

"So why doesn't he?" he said, with his defenses back up.

Because He won't take it. You have to hand it to Him. He says to you, *give it to me. In reality, it's not yours anymore, it's mine. I own it. I paid for it on the Cross – now square up and hand it over. I know where to put it."*

It starts with us deciding which wolf we feed, and it ends with Jesus sealing the deal.

Finally, brothers and sisters, whatever is true, whatever is noble, whatever is right, whatever is pure, whatever is lovely, whatever is admirable—if anything is excellent or praiseworthy—think about such things.

Day forty-three
JESUS, THE RETURNING KING

He'll be back. When He comes, it will be at a time when dark is at its darkest, and the light of the Church is at its brightest. Make no mistake about it, Jesus is not coming back as a last-minute, nick-of-time rescuer. He is coming for His church triumphant, and He is coming to rule.

When last He made a triumphal entry, it was on a colt, but His next entry will be on a charger, a white horse that will put all other horses to shame. There, at the end of days will ride a Jew on a horse. Every eye will turn to Him and know who He is and what He is about to do. No man will oppose Him, or even try. He is back on the soil He trod for thirty-three years, in the land He claimed even before the Abrahamic Covenant.

He will rule without opposition. It will be good because under His leadership it cannot help but be good. Welcome to the Millennial Reign of Jesus. It will be a time in which the earth itself is healed. The earth, after groaning and suffering from defilement and poor stewardship will again thrive. It will be a time of joy, a time of perfect brotherhood and a time without contradiction. In time, under His rule, the word *war* will fall out of use, as well as words like suspicion, fear, hate and divorce.

We try to imagine utopian life, and many have attempted to create it. None have succeeded, and none will, until the day Jesus sets up His government. We can try to express what this will look like, but we will fail to capture its beauty and essence. So, let's try this, below is a short list of what will not be in the government of Jesus.

- most lawyers will be out of business.
- there will be no prisons, half-way houses or rehab clinics.
- hospitals will be museums.
- there will be no passwords – no need for protection from theft, malice or paranoia.
- doors will be manufactured without locks.
- there will be no need for welfare or other assistance programs.

That's the short list. Today's homework is to add ten items – or a thousand. Have fun.

Day forty-four
JESUS IS THE WAY

It's easier to deflect a defect than it is to contemplate it. We spin it, rationalize it, justify it and even ignore it because quite honestly, facing a defect is not fun. Still, there is something in us that is aware that we need redeeming. For many people, it's a nuisance, like a mosquito in the pup tent. In a word, it is this, *we have sinned and are short of the glory of God.* Deep down, we know that if God is going to invite us into an agreeable afterlife, we should do something to make ourselves worthy.

Ancient man knew it, and he was willing to try almost anything short of dying to set things right. There emerged a variety of ideas on how to do this, from pantheism to new age to Buddhism to syncretism, and sadly, people still gravitate to whatever seems to be the most convenient and most culturally acceptable. The sales pitch is for inclusion, and the slogan that justifies it is the popular mantra that *there are many ways up the mountain.* It is relativism, a popular and persuasive idea that works fine for civics or skinning a cat or even climbing a mountain - but it cannot work in the pursuit of absolute truth.

Our culture insists that everyone can enjoy his own truth, but it misappropriates the very meaning of truth. Man can enjoy his own opinion, but that is light-years away from any description of truth. In the end, there is nothing wrong with there being *one way* – in fact, there is everything right with it. God's plan does not lack. He does not need His Way to be updated or renovated. His Way is perfect and cannot be improved upon because His way cost Him everything. Do we think for a moment that there was another way, perhaps an easier and less dramatic way to redeem humankind? Did God elect to elected to sacrifice His Son because it would make a better story? Nonsense! It was the only plausible way to get the job done. The story was so huge, that the remedy had to be the greatest conceivable sacrifice – God Himself.

Still, man insists on choices. When Jesus said *I am the way*, He left no room for qualification, but still we try. We live in a society obese with the notion of entitlement, and we have been conditioned to find a thing objectionable simply because it claims to be *the only thing*. We want to see the menu. We want to go to the theological buffet and pick the belief that most closely conforms to our idea of comfort. All the while, there remains the original item on the menu. It is the living water. It is beautiful Jesus, who tells us, *whoever drinks the water I will give him, will never thirst again.*

Day forty-five
JESUS, THE TRUTH, part one

There is no such thing as a counterfeit $3 bill because there is no such thing as a real $3 bill. In the same way, there cannot be a lie without first having a truth to come against. Because of that, the root of a lie is not an original thing, it exists only as a distortion of truth. In short, if there was no such thing as 'truth' there would be no such thing as a lie. It is the only real weapon the enemy has, and he has spent his fury trying to distract us from truth. Think about it - if the enemy spends all his time coming against *truth* – imagine how majestic that truth must be!

I have a friend who went to work at a local bank as a teller. On her first day she was told that if she accepted any counterfeit bills, it would cost her, and for a short while it was worrisome. I asked her how long it took her to spot counterfeits, and she said, "Two days."

It amazed me, and I asked, "How did you learn it so fast?"

"I didn't," she laughed. "I just got so used to handling the real thing, that the counterfeit identified itself."

There is a world of difference between what seems to be 'most right', and truth. People often say, what is true for you is not necessarily true for me, but what they mean is *opinion*, not truth. If it is eternal truth, it is valid for all, like it or not.

Truth is not a 'thing' or a 'condition' or even a belief. It is the actual essence of the eternal, the reality that had no beginning and will have no end. It is undisturbed by the physical world. There is nothing that can make it less than it is or make it more than it is. Truth exists whether or not anybody exists to think about it or observe it. Finally, truth excludes its opposite. God is infinite, and it is foolishness to think that two infinities could occupy the same space. The singular and sublime demonstration of truth is embodied in Jesus of Nazareth, who came in the flesh.

Hear, O Israel. The LORD our God, the LORD is one.

Day forty-six
JESUS IS THE TRUTH, part two

Truth exists whether or not anybody observes it. Truth never leaves, breaks down, decays or changes. Unlike a lie, truth cannot be added to or deducted from. It is constant, confidant and entirely self-satisfied.

- Truth excludes its opposite. It holds up to rigorous inquiry.
- Truth is *not* a list of options. It is not an opinion.
- It cannot change or be altered in any way and it must be valid for all time past and all-time future.
- It cannot favor one culture, race, sex, age, language or level of understanding.
- It is an equal opportunity essence.
- It is a reality. It is to be discovered, not invented.
- It can never be bullied or intimidated. It cannot back down.
- It is often mocked because of its refusal to change. It is called intolerant, but that is the great beauty of it.
- If the universe ceased to exist, truth would be the residue.

Anything powerful enough to be defined as 'absolute' comes dangerously close to a god-concept, and for many people this is inconvenient, hence the attraction to things being relative.

The relativist, by definition, cannot believe in absolute black or white – and yet the relativist is compelled to respect all the shades of grey in between. It is a mindset that keeps God at a distance, because the very essence of God is the embodiment of absolutes. The result is, these people are compelled to believe in something less, which would be, logically, less than absolute. C.S. Lewis said: *If you look for truth, you may find comfort in the end; if you look for comfort you will not get either comfort or truth only soft soap and wishful thinking in the beginning, and in the end, despair.*

Jesus is Truth. And in this Truth is Life – abundant.

Day forty-seven
JESUS, THE LIFE

I am the expression of the singular Way, in which I am the embodiment of the utmost Truth that promises abundant Life. John 14:6: (expanded)

We have come full cycle. We exist as an expression of God's love. We possess the breathtaking attribute that allows us to be aware of our own condition and mortality, and it is only natural that we would learn all we can about our destiny. It would be reasonable to seek out whatever it is that gives us the greatest return over the longest period of time. In this, the practical, logical and most wonderful solution is to attach ourselves to a good God, who already loves us with an extravagant love.

As a review, Jesus brought victory with Him. He was an invasion force of one, and there was nothing the enemy could do to Him. The enemy had nothing on Him. There was no place to grab ahold, no place to set his hooks, no weak spots for him to infect with a stronghold. Jesus demonstrated His authority over the enemy, then he turned to his disciples (you and me) and said, do what you see me doing, because in Me, there is life.

People who step into this reality, confess that they cannot conceive of a life without this knowledge. It is the knowledge and wisdom that takes a person into victory, and it is this divine contentment that lets that person – with his final breath – know the only thing left to do is to die.

For years, I served on staff at a small-town church. The town was small enough that our sanctuary was often used for funerals of people who did not profess a relationship with Jesus. The funerals were grim, sorrowful displays of despair and resentment. I cannot help but compare that scene to a service celebrating the life of a saint. The difference is night and day, a fitting picture of the Kingdom.

I'm tempted to request that my own memorial service be short and sweet. Joe – who might outlive me – will read a note in my own words; *I'm in heaven and you're not, so neener, neener. You're dismissed. You are now free to move about the Kingdom.*

Why not! Praise Jesus.

Day forty-eight
BREAKFAST BY THE SEA

I'm alone in a boat. I'm not in any peril, just drifting toward shore when I see Him motioning to me. It's Jesus, the Resurrected One, the Victor, my Redeemer. I row to shore and join Him at a little fire He'd kindled. He is making breakfast just for me without the nuisance of a crowd, or even the clutter of disciples.

We talk, at least I think we do, but even when we don't, I bathe in His presence as Master-Savior. He reciprocates by relishing my position as a child of the High King. During our time on the beach, the overpowering essence is this – I don't want to be anywhere else. I don't want it to end, and apparently neither does He. It is clear that He is in no hurry to be somewhere else. As the morning moves along, it comes to me that I am experiencing a foreshadowing of euphoria. For the first time in my recollection, I am aware of the absence of a contrary thought. How does that happen? What is it that makes the smudges and the friction, and the business of the inferior realm disappear? On that beach, there is nothing of the world that could compete with His presence.

This is my place. Breakfast by the sea with my incomparably beautiful Savior. For now, I have to settle for moments of perfect contentment – knowing that it is just a foretaste of glory divine.

His name is Master, Savior, Lion of Judah
Blessed prince of Peace
Shepherd, Fortress, Rock of salvation,
lamb of God is He…
…Son of David, King of the Ages, Eternal Life
Holy God of Glory, his name is Life.

from Carman

Day forty-nine
JESUS IS…

…the Almighty One * the Alpha and Omega * our Advocate and the Author and Perfecter of our faith. He is the Authority * the Bread of Life * the Beloved Son of God * the Bridegroom and the Chief Cornerstone. Jesus is our Deliverer * the One who is Faithful and True * He is the Good Shepherd * the Great High Priest and the Head of the Church. He is the One Before the Beginning * the Famous One and the Rock. * He is the Irresistible One * the Lord of all * the Son of David * the Lion of Judah and the Prevenient One. He is Immanuel * the King of Kings * the Messiah * the Light of the World * the Mediator and our Hope. Jesus is our Redeemer * the Risen Lord * the Son of Man * the Victorious One and the True Vine. Jesus is Wonderful, Counselor, Mighty God and the Prince of Peace. He is our Savior * Redeemer * The Finisher and our Ransom. He is the Way, the Truth and the Life…and He is the Returning King.

Here is your chance to add at least ten ways to Love our Savior. I'll spot you the first one:

1	He is the Bright and Morning Star
2
3
4
5
6
7
8
9
10

Day fifty
SING THE SONG, CHILDREN

Blessed assurance, Jesus is mine!
Oh, what a foretaste of glory divine!
Heir of salvation, purchase of God,
Born of His Spirit, washed in His blood.

This is my story, this is my song,
Praising my Savior all the day long;
This is my story, this is my song,
Praising my Savior all the day long.

> Fanny Crosby

Made in the USA
Columbia, SC
30 June 2022